Murder & Foul Deeds Around

MARGATE

RAMSGATE & BROADSTAIRS

By

D J BIRKIN

To Paul,
Happy Birthday,
Michael

Copyright. © D J BIRKIN 2023 The right of Deborah Birkin to be identified as Author of this work has been asserted in accordance with the Copyright, Designers and Patents Act 1988

All rights reserved. No part of this publication may be reproduced, stored in a retrieval system, or transmitted, in any form or by any means, digital, electronic, mechanical, photocopying, recording or otherwise, without the prior permission in writing of the publisher.

Contents

Introduction 5
1. Gibbeted at St Nicholas at Wade 1609 7
2. The Murdering Squire 1652 11
3. Ramsgate Infanticide 1675 26
4. Wife Hangs Drunken Husband 1773 28
5. Lady Tramp Raped to Death 1786 30
6. The Murder of John Ancell 1786 36
7. The Murder of Thomasine Ward 1807 40
8. The Bizarre Death of Eleanor Tritton 1821 46
9. Strangled Baby on Ramsgate Beach 1863 50
10. The Ramsgate Serial killer 1865 52
11. Murder by Salmestone Grange 1876 71
12. The Baby down the Toilet 1878 81
13. Dead on the Beach at Margate 1880 87
14. Tragedy in a Northwood Cottage 1886 91
15. Richardson the Spree Shooter 1888 98
16. The Murder of Little Milly Merriman 1891 105
17. Who Killed Mrs Noel 1893 113
18. The Broadstairs Parcel Bomb 1893 140
19. Suicide. Are you Joking? 1893 145
20. Slaughter of the Garlinge Babies 1894 149

21. The Baby in the Locked Tin Box 1895 158
22. Thrown off Dumpton Gap 1897 162
23. Failed Murder at Margate 1902 169
24. Attack on Margate Ice Cream Boy 1903 171
25. He Blew up his Son with Dynamite 1903 174
26. Was Charlotte Turk a Ghost? 1903 184
27. Margate Husband Kills Wife 1905 189
28. Ramsgate Hotel Throat Slashing 1912 192
29. The murder of Sarah Brockman 1914 194
30. The Dead Baby in the Cupboard 1915 204
31. The Chinese Lantern Café 1927 208
32. Matricide at the Metropole 1929 221
33. Who Murdered Margery Wren? 1930 235
34. Attempted Gassing 1935 259
35. The Birchington Corpse 1938 261
36. Scarred for Life 1940 273
37. Minster Child Sexually Abused 1940 274
38. She didn't like Boys 1941 275
39. Wicked Mother Drowned her Son 1946 279
40. Copper tries to kill Wife 1947 281
41. Husband hits wife with Axe 1949 284
42. The Broadstairs Flasher 1950 286
43. She threw her Babies in the Harbour 1950 287
44. The Murder of Lillian Chubb 1958 289

Introduction

Welcome my fellow murder sleuths, thank you for your interest. In this book we will take a look at some of the historic murders and foul deeds that have taken place in an area of Kent known as 'Thanet'. Even if you have never heard of this area there cannot be an English person alive that has not heard of Thanet's principal town, Margate.

Once celebrated as the Blackpool of the South, Margate will forever be synonymous with donkey rides, golden sands, kiss-me-quick hats, sticks of rock and of course Chas and Dave's 80's classic the Margate song. But as memorable as "Margit" is, there are two other towns in Thanet with an equally rich history of their own - Ramsgate and Broadstairs. These three small seaside towns have given us some fascinating murders, some solved but others so mysterious that even today the police are still baffled.

I spent over a year researching these cases so I hope you enjoy my compilation, which I can assure you is the most comprehensive account of Thanet murder cases compiled in print to date. There are 44 cases recounted in as much detail as I could unearth and I have also included new research by myself into the villain's and victim's family trees.

The earliest murder case I've recorded for Thanet occurred in 1609. The details are scant, but because of the guilty man's sentence I thought it worth recording for its local interest.

Dedicated to Wally

1.

Gibbeted at St Nicholas at Wade 1609

At Rochester Assizes on 20th July 1609. John Lee, of St Nicholas-At-Wade in the Island of Thanet, was found guilty of murdering Ralph Chillenden, aged 31, in St Nicholas-At-Wade village - John Lee had bashed his victim's head in with a hedge stake on 1st June 1609.

Ralph Chillenden's wounds were so severe that he languished only a few hours, dying before daybreak.

John Lee was indicted on the 4 June 1609 at an inquest held in St Nicholas-At-Wade village (most likely in an ale house then known as the Hare and Hounds, not the modern day pub.) Lee was sentenced to be taken from Rochester gaol, where he had been held after being convicted at his trial at Rochester Assizes, down to Canterbury and there be publicly hanged. Oaten Hill Green outside the old Nunnery gates was the usual place.

It was ordered by the Judge that after the execution Lee's body was to be taken to St Nicholas-At-Wade village and there be displayed in chains (gibbeted) at the side of the main road close to the scene of his crime. No exact spot was mentioned for the murder scene but it is a small village so anywhere on the main road in or out would have been the ideal position to attract the maximum amount of people to view Lee's corpse.

The victim's family were wealthy yeoman stock living in the Canterbury area. This chosen sentence meant they could attend the hanging on mass without having to travel all the way to Rochester again as they had done for the trial.

So why was this murderer gibbeted and not simply hanged and buried? Well, by murdering Ralph Chillenden, John Lee had committed the more serious crime of petty treason. He had murdered his master and therefore someone superior to himself.

In law, in that period, persons superior to others included a husband being superior to a wife, a clergyman to a layman, a master to an employee or servant and obviously any member of the upper classes, especially with a title. Working class women were at the bottom of the heap as all men were superior to them.

I did some research for Ralph Chillenden and found he was indeed from a very wealthy land owning family. He was baptised at Boughton-under-Blean near Canterbury 24th Dec 1578 the son of a Yeoman farmer named John Chillenden. Ralph had a large extended family in the Canterbury area with many uncles & cousins who were all land owners. He had nine siblings, some of whom died young: Thomas 1577, Margaret 1580, Susan 1583, Ann 1585, William 1587, John 1588, Edward(1) 1589, Edward(2) 1590 and Alice 1592. Ralph Chillenden was buried on the 5th June 1609 at Boughton-under-Blean church.

Why John Lee murdered his master I couldn't find out, neither could I find any other murders in this little village so perhaps the gibbeting of John Lee did act as a worthwhile deterrent.

In 1834, Britain outlawed gibbeting completely. Tradesmen and the public had begun to complain that the sight and smell of rotting corpses was detrimental to trade. The public, especially the ladies, had no desire to see such spectacles when out shopping - and who wants to take their kids for a walk by the sea and give their little darlings nightmares from seeing a smelly rotting corpse in a cage.

Sources for the murder of Ralph Chillenden:
Calendar of Assize Records Kent Indictments King James 1.
plus Ancestry.com for the family research.

THE BLOODY HUSBAND, AND CRVELL NEIGHBOVR.

Or,

A True Historie

Of

TWO MVRTHERS,

Lately committed in *Laurence* Parish, in the Isle of *Thanet* in *Kent*, neer *Sandwich* :

One Murther

By the hands of *Adam Sprackling* Esquire, who upon the 12th day of *December* last, being Sabbath day; in the morning, cut, mangled, and murthered his own wife; for which fact he was hanged at *Sandwich* upon Wednesday the 27th day of *April* last, 1653.

The other

The Murther of *Richard Langly*, of the same Parish, whose blood also (as is here shewed) cryed against the said Mr. *Sprackling*,

---

Numbers 35. 33. *Blood defileth the Land, and the Land cannot be clensed of the blood that is shed therein, but by the blood of him that shed it.*

Written by one that lives neer the Place where the said Murthers were committed, and was present at Mr. *Sprackling's* tryall; And published for the warning, and good of all.

May 13. 1653. *Imprimatur,*
Edm. Calamy *May. 19.*

LONDON,
Printed by *Tho. Warren.* 1653.

2.

The Murdering Squire 1652

In gallows field, just outside the town wall of Sandwich (now a picnic area!) a huge crowd once assembled to watch the execution of a member of the local gentry. The public came from miles around, some as far as London, with estimates of 30,000 or more spectators jostling for the best view. It was always a treat for the ragged class to witness one of the nobs get their comeuppance with the added attraction of ogling the attending gentry's fine clothing and conveyances. - the pickpockets always had a field day.

Escorted to the gallows, his step unfaltering, his long fair hair and velvet cloak billowing in the wind, the condemned gentleman forbade any clergy to come near him. Squire Sprackling was tall, handsome, and cavalier in both his bearing and mode, he met his end defiantly.

Within days of the execution, a now very rare pamphlet in the British Library was being offered for sale in Kent & London. It was entitled:

'The Bloody Husband and Cruell Neighbour or, A Truth Historie of Two Murthers' It's authorship, "By one that lives near the place where said murthers were committed.' It is dated 1653.

(Note the period use of the word murther for murder)

This case came to my attention when a neighbour was talking of her interest in local ghost legends. She informed me that the pitiful cries of a woman named Katherine Sprackling could be heard coming from tunnels, supposedly, still beneath Ellington Park near Ramsgate.

Now, I personally do not believe in ghosts, until I see one with my own eyes I suppose, but I do believe that the foundations for such legends are nearly always rooted in true events that have been embroidered with the passing of time.

Intrigued, I set myself to find what truths, if any, lay behind the urban legend of the Ellington Park ghost.

Ellington ark lies just westward of Ramsgate on the edge of the village of St Lawrence. It was purchased by the local council in 1892, its grounds to be used as a public pleasure park. The once grand mansion, Ellington House, much neglected having been tenanted out as a farmhouse by then, was demolished by the council in 1896 and only its foundations survive today.

The seat in this rural idyll had, since the 13th century, been held by a family of the name of Ellington, who passed it to the ancient Kent family of Thatcher. Then in 1558, Sir Adam Sprackling, a native of Thanet and one time steward to Queen Elizabeth, purchased the estate and bequeathed it to one of his sons, Robert Sprackling, who, declining to live there himself installed there one of his own son's also named Adam Sprackling after his well respected Grandfather.

The old pamphlet of 1653 describes Ellington place as consisting of 'luxuriant corn fields and fertile meadows.'

Now it is with this Adam Sprackling that the legend begins.

Adam Sprackling was typical of too many of his class. He had never needed to work. His fortune had been handed him on the proverbial silver platter. He was the local squire and could do what he liked. An arrogant wastrel, Adam considered the estate could run itself and his only duty was to please himself and this he did throughout his adult life, terrorising the neighbourhood villages of Thanet, swearing, boozing, gambling, whoring and generally attacking and thrashing anyone that defied him or spoke out against his riotous behaviour. Adam was always out of control and a law unto himself.

In 1631, Adam had married the daughter of a wealthy gent, Sir Robert Lewknor of Acrise Place nr Folkestone, a former High Sheriff of Kent, and his wife Mary Harmon. The marriage had probably been arranged by the parents for mutual financial benefit. Adam was aged 26 and so was his bride Katherine Lewknor. Both had been born in 1605, he at St Lawrence Thanet, she at Acrise Folkestone. Initially the marriage was amicable enough, and Katherine bore four children; Robert 1633, Margaret 1635, Adam 1637 and Mary 1638 who died within months. Sadly, domestic bliss was not to Adam's taste and he continued his old bachelor habits. Describing his ways in the old pamphlet of 1653 'he did ride about the Island (Thanet) and frequent Tap houses (pubs) and there rant and roar, game and swear exceedingly.'

Ellington House, refaced and modernised in the 18th century

In contrast his wife, Katherine Sprackling, was said to be attractive, good natured and extremely pious. She accepted her married lot with fair grace and raised her three surviving children like a good God fearing Mother. Her husband on the other hand was Godless and getting deeper into debt. His creditors were always after him, and he dealt with them in his usual manner, by bullying, thrashing, and even shooting at them whenever they dared press him for money. Frequently drunk and always in bad temper as

Adam was, the pious Katherine was often forced to flee her husband's beatings and lock herself away in her own home. Sprackling was also renowned for holding grudges against anyone who crossed him.

Richard Langley was a respected deputy to the Mayor of Sandwich. In 1648, he and two others, Edward Taddy the parish constable, and Humphrey Pudner deputy to the Mayor of Dover, were ordered by the Mayor of Sandwich to go and disarm Adam Sprackling. It appears he had been threatening someone again, probably a debt collector. Sprackling was duly taken in a tavern in the parish of St John's Ramsgate. He put up a fight but was eventually overpowered and served a brief few weeks sentence in Canterbury Castle Gaol. This incident only fuelled Adam's temper. He wanted revenge on Langley, Pudner and Taddy for having had the audacity to arrest him.

After his release, Sprackling made a point of seeking out Taddy and giving him a sound beating. When it came to Richard Langley, Sprackling cornered him with his sword and warned him in front of witnesses that he was going to kill him. A few days later Richard Langley was found dead, laying at the side of the road in a pool of his own blood, he had been shot in the back. Adam Sprackling was obviously suspected for the murder.

On the day of his death, Langley had been out drinking with friends when he heard that Adam Sprackling, in the company of two of his pals, Paul Allen and Thomas Emerson, were fired up with alcohol and out to get him. Langley fled and sought refuge with a friend, John Johnson, who provided him with a horse to speed his escape from the area. Johnson later recalled that no sooner had Langley taken up his mount when Sprackling spotted him and chased him out of Ramsgate. No more was seen of poor Richard Langley until his bloody corpse was discovered.

Paul Allen and Thomas Emerson immediately went on the run. Later that same year Emerson was captured and hanged at Canterbury in 1648 for his part in Langley's murder. He did not grass on his friends. Paul Allen was never seen again and Adam Sprackling was not even arrested. (No doubt the local constables didn't fancy themselves being found shot in the back.) Once again Adam Sprackling had done what he liked and gotten away with it. He must have thought he was invulnerable.

Come the winter of 1652, the Ellington estate was in want. There was little money coming in and Adam was deeper in debt than ever. His sanity was also now in question. Constantly drunk and always vicious, he openly fornicated with his female servants and invited labourers to drink with him inside Ellington house, which he kept barricaded to keep his creditors at bay.

His loyal and loving wife, Katherine, was now confined in this violent house of abuse. Her husband often used her as a release for his anger and frustration causing her to be frequently harmed.

Eventually on the night of Saturday December 11th 1652, the dire situation in Ellington Place took a sinister turn.

Adam was drunk as usual, he had spent the evening drinking with a neighbour named Lamming. At around 10pm he sent for a sailor of his acquaintance named Knowler in Ramsgate instructing him to come to the house at once. Luckily, in hindsight, Knowler refused, saying he was already in bed.

Sprackling then did the same to an elderly tenant of his named Martin, who was also in bed, but dutifully did as his squire bid him and went to the kitchen of Ellington House.

It was now the early hours of Sunday morning, the 12th of December.

In the kitchen, Martin found Sprackling, his wife Katherine, Lamming and a house servant named Ewell. Martin was not wise as to why he had been sent for. Sprackling now openly accused Katherine of conspiracy with the bailiffs saying she was deliberately leaving doors to the house open. Katherine sat calmly as she took yet another barrage of verbal abuse. 'Her words to him,' claims the old pamphlet, 'were full of loving and sweet expression.' In response, Sprackling struck her in the face with the hilt of his dagger. Lamming rose up, quickly excused himself, and hastily left.

Sprackling continued to berate his wife in the presence of the servants Ewell & Martin. Ewell was now very drunk and Martin too was being plied with liquor. Soon, Katherine, no doubt tired and fearing for her safety, had had enough and she rose to leave the room. No sooner had she placed her hand on the kitchen door when Sprackling attacked her. Grabbing a meat cleaver, he swung it at her hand. Katherine collapsed, her wrist completely cut through, the bone severed, her hand hanging down, attached only by a slither of skin.

For a long time Adam had been delusional. Now fuelled with alcohol and boiling with self perceived grievances, he had convinced himself that it was Katherine who was the sole cause of his downfall. He hated her. All evening he had planned to kill her for her, imagined, disloyalty to him.

The servant, Ewell, was too drunk, or scared, to do anything. Martin was too old to intervene. Instead Martin implored his mistress to be quiet, that the situation might still be well as he wrapped a kitchen cloth around his mistress's severed wrist.

Eventually, Katherine pulled herself to her knees and prayed aloud to God to forgive her sins and those of her husband's, for she surely forgave him for what he had just done.

This only seemed to anger the Godless Sprackling all the more, and in one strike he brought down the chopper on Katherine's head, cleaving it in two and spilling her brains, she dropped to the floor stone dead.

Adam was delighted. The first part of his drunken plan had been executed. Now for part two. Adam fetched six of his dogs and killed them, throwing their lifeless bodies on top of his wife's corpse. (why the dogs?) Then he ordered the terrified Martin to help him tie up the drunken Ewell and smear his Mistress's blood all over the servant, announcing. "We will blame it on Ewell, say he has gone mad." (Still I see no reason for the killing of six dogs.) Martin, now in complete fear for his own life, did as his master bid him. Sprackling then made his escape down through the trapdoor in the kitchen floor and into the wine cellars beneath.

It has long been claimed that the cellars of Ellington Place lead to tunnels used to smuggle in contraband goods. These tunnels, it is claimed, were dug by Sprackling's labourers and extend as far as Pegwell Bay, a favourite smugglers landing beach approximately 1.6 miles distant, but more likely just as far as the church or a nearby inn. There are probably some grains of truth to this legend of the tunnels, if not their length, as it would have been even more stupid of Sprackling to have incarcerated himself in a cellar with no means of escape when he could simply have left by the back door.

Ewell, no doubt frightened into soberness, now made his own escape and raised the alarm. Soon a posse of local officials were in hot pursuit of Sprackling. One account says Sprackling was taken whilst hiding in a tunnel armed with a pistol and sword. Another simply that he was apprehended some distance away. Either way, Sprackling was captured, bound up, and carried to a nearby boat.

At that time St Lawrence village came under the jurisdiction of the Cinque port of Sandwich and so it was to that town Sprackling was taken by boat and, once there, locked up in Sandwich gaol.

The coroner's inquest into Katherine's death was held the next day. Consequently, old Martin was then arrested under suspicion of aiding Sprackling in the murder of Katherine and for trying to implicate the servant Ewell.

Katherine Sprackling was solemnly buried three days later on the 15th of December in St Laurence's Church. (The village takes its name from the church and has acquired a difference in spelling, St Lawrence.)

Now that Sprackling was caught, with little chance of being set free, many local folk plucked up the courage to come forward and give statements of the many vicious deeds Adam had committed.

One man told of a violent disagreement between Adam and a John Simmons in a pub which ended in Simmons being

pinned to the wall with Adam's rapier. Another witness had seen Adam beaten in a fist-fight with a man named Robert Lister, so Adam, in return, had employed a man named Corslet to give Lister a good beating. One chap named William Grant told how Sprackling had cleaved his head with a cutlass and he was lucky to have survived. Even respected Law Officers admitted that Sprackling had often fired off his pistols at them, threatening to kill them if they reported him. It would seem the whole neighbourhood had lived in fear of Adam Sprackling for decades.

Squire Sprackling was held in Sandwich gaol for four months, until the April assizes, plenty of time for the Mayor to amass a large body of evidence against him.

The trial finally took place at Sandwich's Guildhall on Friday 22nd April 1653 before a packed audience.

A Mr Peter Peak, opening for the prosecution, spoke of the 'crying sin of murther' and how such acts were a 'land-defiling and God provoking sin'. The court then received the Bill of Indictment presented by Katherine's brother, Steward Lewknor.

Sprackling tried to delay the proceedings by objecting to every man on the jury. Nevertheless, he was ignored and the jury was sworn in. Sprackling pleaded not guilty. He claimed he was out of his mind at that time and had not meant to kill his wife. He then called two physicians to confirm his mental instability. They failed to convince the jury. Adam then called several servants of his wife, each of whom swore that their master was indeed mad. But the court wasn't having any of it. Sprackling had planned to kill his wife, it was clearly premeditated by his actions that night. The murder of Richard Langley was also brought up and witnesses recounted Sprackling's part in that crime. No one had a good word to say in support of Adam. He was a hated man.

The jury quickly found Sprackling guilty of the wilful murder of his wife Katherine and he was sentenced to death. The charges against the servant Martin were dropped. When asked by the Judge if Sprackling had any reply to his sentence? Adam responded 'No man can judge between man and wife, but God alone!' (It seems he believed in God when it suited him)

On Wednesday the 27th April 1653, Sprackling was hanged in Gallows field Sandwich. Afterwards, says the old pamphlet, "And after stripped, and layd forth, and coffined at the Sign of the "Three Kings" in Sandwich;

and the next day towards night carried from thence six miles on men's shoulders over the Ferry to St Lawrence Church."

I then researched some additional information and compiled a Sprackling family tree for those with a family interest.

After Adam's death, Ellington Place passed to his youngest son, also named Adam Sprackling, a fellow of Peter house college, Cambridge. The eldest son Robert must have inherited other property.

The Ellington estate must have been held in trust for Adam junior as he was only 15 at the time. He then sold it to the Troward family, who were cousins of the Spracklings. His sister Margaret Sprackling, daughter of Adam and Katherine, then married one of the Troward cousins and so the house came back into the direct family. Not surprisingly, as her Mother was murdered in the place, Margaret didn't want the house. Eventually it descended to one of her husband's relatives Mr. William Troward, son of Edward Troward of Manston Green. Troward died in 1767. Ellington estate then passed to his two nieces, the daughters of his sister, Sarah Troward, who had married Alban Spencer, gent. The daughters were Susan Spencer, wife of Robert Buck, Mercer, of London, and Mary Spencer, the wife of Robert Gunsley Ayerst, clerk, of Canterbury.

Ellington House then became a tenanted farm until sold to the local council in 1892.

It is interesting to note; Margaret Sprackling had many descendants one being the famous author Rumer Godden OBE author of the novel Black Narcissus (film 1947)

A book published in 1895 by Charles Cotton, entitled History & Antiquities of the Church and Parish of St Laurence (Lawrence), Thanet (Ramsgate) speaks of repairs to the church as well as archaeological investigations done at the church in the 1890's. One entry is most interesting! It reads:

"At the north east angle of the north west pier and interred in an angular direction north east and south west, about eighteen inches under the level of the floor, we found the skeleton of a man between 6 and 7 feet in height; who he was and why buried in this manner will probably ever remain a mystery: but it may have been the remains of MR ADAM SPRACKLING who was (is reputed to have been) buried on Thursday the 28th of April 1653 in St Laurence Church, see "The Bloody Husband" where in the night he was buried (secretly) near his wife", and as there is no entry in the Burial Register of this Mr Adam Sprackling's burial (although that of his wife is duly recorded) – it seems probable that it was he who was thus hastily interred, especially as the burial was in the passage way. The other vaults in the Church were not disturbed.

Sprackling line of descent:

Gulielmus Sprackling b1460-1569 at Thanet Kent

Children of Gulielmus:

Nicholas Sprackling 1484-1569 who married Isabel Oxenden

Children of Nicholas & Isabel Oxenden:

Robert Sprackling 1515-1590 who married Constance. Also sons Luke, John & Leonard & daughter Alice. (info; family tombstone in St Laurence)

Children of Robert & Constance

Sir Adam Sprackling (knt) 1553-1610 who married Katherine Estday (Dame) 1558-1627 married at Saltwood 1576 Her father was John Estday of Hythe. Also sons Nicholas, Luke & John plus 5 daughters, Marie, Eve, Margaret, Judith & Rachel (info; family tombstone in St Laurence)

Children of Sir Adam & Dame Katherine Estday:

Robert Sprackling 1577-1646 who married Margaret Moyle, other children: Katherine's tombstone in St Laurence church lists 7 sons & 10 daughters) Robert (as above) Plus Adam (of Fordwich see note below), John, Henry (1) Henry(2) Charles, Thomas, Judeth, Elizabeth, Katheren(1), Mary, Annis, Katheren(2) Margery, Frances, Margret, Hanna. (Old spellings)

NOTE: Adam Sprackling of Fordwich married Ann Haymen daughter of Henry Hayman Esq of Sellinge. They had issue: Robert, Henry, Katherine, Rebecca. The wife, Ann died in 1659, and was buried at Chilham.

He is not the same Adam Sprackling in this murder case, and not of Ellington Place.

Children of Robert Sprackling & Margaret Moyle: at Thanet

Adam Sprackling 1605-1653 Baptised 20 March 1605/6 at St Lawrence Thanet Kent. He had married Katherine Lewknor b1605, marriage at Acrise Folkestone 21 July 1631,

Other children of Robert Sprackling and therefore siblings of Adam Sprackling; Katherine 1599-1607, Maria ?, Margaret 1611, Robert 1615, & Margery 1615 (twin) who married 1st: William Abbott in 1637 at Temple Ewell Dover and 2nd: James Rigden in 1653 at St Laurence Ramsgate. (info from family tombstones in St Laurence Church Ramsgate)

Children of Adam Sprackling & Katherine Lewknor

Robert 1633, Margaret 1635, Adam 1637, Mary 1638-1639

Katherine Sprackling, maiden name Lewknor, daughter of (Sir) Robert Lewknor (1588-1636), & his wife Mary Hamon. He was the Son of Sir Edward Lewknor & Susan Heigham.

Sir Robert Lewknor married Mary (daughter and coheir of Alexander Hamon of Acrise, Kent), by whom he had five children which included Katherine.

Sir Robert Lewknor inherited the manor of Kingston Buci, Sussex but also inherited the manor of Acrise nr Folkestone from his father-in-law.

Robert Lewknor (1588-1636) was Knighted in 1607 and made High Sheriff of Kent in 1630.

See; Wikipedia, Edward Lewknor (his father) for additional Lewknor family.

With regard to the other men involved in Richard Langley's death:

Thomas Emerson: Hanged at Oaten Hill Canterbury in 1648 for involvement in the murder of Richard Langley. It is still not clear which of the three men actually shot Langley. Emerson was born in St Lawrence in 1612 the Son of Robert Emerson & Jane Angram. In 1634 he married Ann Luckett. She was left a widow with three young children: Robert 1638, Anne 1641, John 1643.

Paul Allen: Unfortunately there were far too many Allen's in Kent at that time, and several family groups in Thanet. I could not find a Paul amongst them that could be directly attributed to the man in this case study, it was noted several times that after absconding he was never seen again and maybe left the country.

Sources: The Bloody Husband and Cruell Neighbour or, A Truth Historie of Two Muthers' 1653. From the British Library.

The history and antiquities, ecclesiastical as well as civil, of the Isle of Tenet (Thanet) in Kent. By John Lewis 1736.

The English Baronetage by Arthur Collins 1741.

The baronetage of England by Rev. William Betham 1803.

Personal research into Thanet parish records. Family search IGI and Ancestry.com. History & Antiquities of the Church and Parish of St Laurence 1895. British newspapers archive online and Sandwich guildhall museum.

So it seems there was actually quite a bit of truth behind the legend of the Ellington Park ghost - but not all of it. Local legend also claims that a servant maid hid the Spracklings' small daughter in a cupboard while Adam tried to smash it open with an axe! The maid and child then escaped into the tunnels (presumably when he wasn't looking & taking an axe rest) and the child was lost, never to be found again. - Obvious poppycock. Robert and Margaret Sprackling were born in 1633 and 1635 and were 19 & 17 when their mother was murdered. Margaret and Robert both married and have modern day living descendants. Adam junior was 15 at the time and away at boarding school (this is verified) - if he married I do not know to whom. The other daughter, Mary, had died a baby shortly after baptism. There are no historic records of any other children born to the Spracklings or reports in contemporary records of any lost children.

3.

Ramsgate Infanticide 1675

On the 16th Aug 1675, Martha Lamminge of Ramsgate, a spinster, appeared before Maidstone Assizes charged that on 1st August 1675 at Ramsgate she did give birth to a male bastard and did strangle it immediately afterwards. Martha was found guilty of infanticide and sentenced to death. She then asked to plead her belly and a jury of matrons were tasked with examining Martha. They found that she was not quick with child (not pregnant) The sentence of hanging therefore could go ahead. She would have been executed on Penenden Heath at Maidstone within two days of sentencing, three if it fell on a Sunday.

Pregnancy was only accepted if foetal movement could be discerned - usually at 3-4 months.

Although not technically impossible for Martha to be pregnant again, she must have been quite stupid, or just desperate, to think that midwives could detect a pregnancy just 16 days after her having given birth.

Source; Calendar of Assize records Kent indictments for King Charles 11

Murder & Foul Deeds Around Margate Ramsgate & Broadstairs

4.

Wife Hangs Drunken Husband 1773

On Friday 11 June 1773 A labouring man by the name of Thomas Settertree, of the Village of Minster in Thanet, came home intoxicated with liquor. His wife, having previously threatened him with death if he ever did so again, tied a rope around the husband's neck and attached it to their bed post. Next morning neighbours, alerted by the family's panicked six children, discovered the hanging husband quite dead with the wife lying beside him in bed. She confessed little regret for his death that she herself had brought upon him. An inquest found Mrs Settertree guilty of petty treason by wilfully murdering her husband. She was taken to St Dunstan's goal at Canterbury to await trial at the next Assizes.

Unfortunately no name was given for the wife.

Records suggest she never made her trial. No woman was tried for murdering her husband in Kent in 1773. We can therefore only speculate that Mrs Settertree either died in prison (gaol fever, typhus, was rampant in the 18thc) or maybe she killed herself. Unless she was deemed to be insane and was unfit to stand trial. Although in such instances the person would still be recorded at the Assizes as insane and sentenced to a prison asylum for an undetermined period. Had she been found guilty of petty treason, the sentence for killing your husband, or another deemed your superior, was to be burnt at the stake on Penenden Heath. (I think I would have topped myself faced with that prospect) Between 1735 & 1799 some 32 women in England were burnt at the stake for murdering their husbands. None were the female subject of this case. The last burning at the stake in Kent itself was that of Margaret Ryan in 1776. Madge Ryan had stabbed her husband Patrick to death.

Note that prior to the 18th century it was not uncommon to actually burn woman alive with some Judges specifying as much but by the early 1700s it was considered more humane to first hang the condemned until dead before burning the corpse although there are a few cases of accidentally burning ladies alive much to the horror of all those who were present. Margaret Onion of Chelmsford Essex suffered such a fate in 1735 when the fire was lit too early and her screams were said to be most pitiful as the panicked executioner tried to knock her out by throwing logs of wood at her head. Whilst on another occasion a merciful executioner managed to kill a screaming woman by beating her in the stomach with a wooden stool before the flames engulfed her.

Source: Stamford Mercury 17 June 1773. Leeds Intelligencer Tuesday 15 June 1773

To read about the actual burnings at the stake that are recorded for 18th century England go to;

http://www.capitalpunishmentuk.org/burning.html

5.

Lady Tramp Raped to Death 1786

It was ten O'clock at night, when a destitute couple left a pub in the village of Minster in Thanet. Homeless wanderers, clothed only in tattered rags, they slowly hobbled past the church of St Mary, and continued down Marsh Farm lane towards the marshes. The man stood out as a foreigner. He had dark hair and an exceptionally long beard. Shaking with the palsy, his steps were aided by a white stick.

For this poor old couple it had been an unusually good evening. Friendly villagers had provided them with a few drinks, all they wanted for now was somewhere to lay their heads down for the night. The weather was dry and very warm, it was June 1786.

Mr Savin soon found a soft grassy spot by a dry ditch, his wife, Mary, curled up under the hedge next to her husband. Soon they were sound asleep in the moonlight.

Two hours later, Mr Savin was startled from his slumber by the screams of his wife. Mary was being dragged out from under the hedge by four men. Mr Savin stumbled to his feet. He was old, feeble, and disabled having only one hand. Bravely the crippled man attempted to pull the youths off of his wife. It was futile. The men were strong and much younger. One of the gang soon knocked him down and pinned Mr Savin to the ground. The other three took it in turns to rape Mary whilst all Mr Savin could do was listen in horror to his wife's screams of 'Murder. Murder.'

And then suddenly the screaming stopped.

Sadly, the ordeal had not ended. The blaggard holding the old man down now wanted his turn to have sex with Mary. His hold on Savin was taken up by another, who then sat on the old man whilst his friend had his wicked enjoyment. Mary made no sound at all.

The lust for their evil deed sated, the four rapists ran off towards the marshes. Old Savin crawled to his wife's side. It was too late. The old lady was obviously dead, her blank eyes staring up at the moon, she had been raped, beaten and throttled.

Stumbling back to the village, shaking and blinded by tears, Savin raised the alarm. Mary's body was found and taken back to the pub.

The Savin's were not residents of the village, although they had visited a few times and were known to a few, they were still tramps and so suspicion now fell upon Savin that he had killed his wife in a drunken fight. Not being able to name the four rapists, old Savin seemed unable to support his story. Locals were weary of him being a foreigner as Savin could speak only broken English and Spanish, but his description of the man that had first held him down suggested he might be telling the truth after all. Savin told how the thug had been clothed in a brown waistcoat and long trousers. He had held a horse bridle in one hand and had the forefinger of his left hand missing. Immediately the name of one John Williams was raised.

Next day an inquest was held in the pub. By daylight the pinch marks and bruises on both sides of Mary's neck could be clearly seen - something a man with only one hand like Savin, could not have done. Then a man who lived in a cottage in Marsh Farm lane came forward. He testified that he had heard a woman's screams of "Murder" plus the voices of several men. He had then opened his bedroom window and heard one voice distinctly say "Damn the old man, keep him down." Now Savin was believed.

The court brought in a quick verdict of wilful murder by persons unknown and a search party was set to find John Williams. Later that day a ferryman, at the Red House on the marshes, told the constable that he had rowed across the fleet, a man answering John William's description. The passenger had seemed greatly agitated. It appeared that Williams had gotten away.

Enquiries found that John Williams had been born at Wingham near Canterbury and the search moved in that direction, in case he should be concealed amongst friends or relatives. Three other men, known to associate with Williams, were arrested and held for further enquiries to be made. The clear description of Williams had him found a few days later, hiding in Romney Marsh. He was put in New Romney lock-up. Later all four men were removed to St. Dunstan's gaol, Canterbury to await trial at the next county assizes, which were to be held in Maidstone in the August.

Minster in Thanet c1800

I found the next part of this case incredibly sad: Savin had been born in Kingston, Jamaica. He was not a Negro, but of Spanish origin. He had lived the life of a British Naval sailor. His wife, Mary, was English and he had met and married her in Jamaica. Some years previous to her horrific murder on the 28th of June, the couple had come to England and Mr Savin had been admitted to the seaman's infirmary at Deal after an accident on board his ship. There his hand had been amputated. This dismissed him from the navy. Released, crippled, with no job and nowhere to go, the couple's life had been reduced to that of distressed tramps. Now with the inquest over, still no one aided the disabled, lonely old man, affording him no option but to just wander away from Minster village to beg for his needs where he could. When the date for the trial was set, old Savin could not be found. Where he had tramped to, no one knew. A description was placed in the Kentish Gazette along with an urgent appeal requesting that anyone knowing of Savin's whereabouts, to come forward. He had last been sighted heading towards Hythe, wearing a greatcoat, much ragged, a round sailors hat and was carrying a long white stick. What happened to the poor broken man is unknown.

Before the trial started, William's confessed to the rape, but refused to name his accomplices. He was an atrociously violent man, a repeat offender who had been imprisoned for other crimes previously in Canterbury. The three other men held under suspicion alongside him all provided "false" alibi's given to them by the farmer that employed them - and obviously wished to retain them come harvesting. Therefore, the judge, reluctantly, had no choice but to dismiss all charges against the three.

Williams on the other hand, again confessed all in court as he had no alibi and was not in the farmer's employ. What he told the court only revolted those that heard it. He stated that, yes, it was he who had held the old man down, whilst the others, whom he did not know! Ravished the old woman. He then took his turn to ravish her, but did not murder her, *she being already dead when he ravished her!*

On Sat 12th of August 1786, at 10am in the morning, John Williams was hanged on Penenden Heath at Maidstone, the county execution ground for Kent. He drew only a small crowd. He said nothing to them. The body was then delivered up to surgeons at Maidstone infirmary for dissection. Common law at the time dictated that criminal's cadavers could be used as teaching aids for medical students.

I could find nothing more of the Savins, regarding their lives, or that of their respected families. It may be that Savin was Mary's surname and not her Spanish husband's name. The Thanet area has many old families by the name of Savin so she could have originally hailed from the area.

Sources: Kentish Gazette 11 July 1786. Hampshire Chronicle 17 July 1786. Northampton Mercury 12 August 1786. Hereford Journal 13 July 1786. Plus other newspapers in the British news archive.

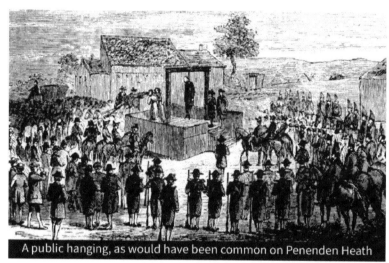

A public hanging, as would have been common on Penenden Heath

John Ancell was murdered in the road near Drapers Hospital Margate. This Charity house for the poor was founded in 1708 by Michael Yoakley

6.

The Murder of John Ancell 1786

On Sunday 9 April 1786 a gruesome discovery was made. A badly smashed up body lay on a Thanet road. The corpse was found near Drapers hospital at Margate and it showed much injury. It was soon discovered that the dead man was a poor local labourer named John Ancell.

John was from a tiny hamlet called Sacketts Hill near St Peters Village by Broadstairs. Enquiries were made so an inquest could be held to determine how the poor fellow had met with such a horrific demise. Information was soon discovered that Ancell had, on the previous evening, been seen drinking in Margate town and was much in liquor. After leaving an alehouse he walked with a friend as far as St John's churchyard and parted with him there at a quarter to eleven. John walked on towards his home in Sacketts Hill. Ancell was observed to be followed shortly after by Charles Twyman on horseback heading in the same direction. Twyman was known to have had a dispute with Ancell some time past which he felt was unsettled. A 12 year old servant boy was with Twyman sitting up behind him on the horse.

Men were sent to question Charles Twyman at his home. He lived with his wife and five young children at a farm named Bromstone near St Peters. (the area of the farm is now Bromstone Road) Charles Twyman could not be found at home, his wife didn't know, or wouldn't tell, where her husband was. It seemed he had gone on the run. The servant boy however, was at Bromstone and was taken into custody and examined. At first the boy denied any knowledge of Ancell's death, but once informed there were witnesses who were prepared to swear they had seen the lad with his Master following Ancell, the boy broke down and confessed all.

He said he was with his Master, Charles Twyman, on horseback as had been stated, and they followed John Ancell as he left Margate. On the road to Sacketts Hill his Master over took Ancell and observed him carrying a bag. Twyman called out in the dark that he was a customs officer and Ancell should hand over the bag. Ancell called back that he knew Twyman's voice and refused to give up his property. Twyman dismounted and a scuffle broke out between the men whereupon Twyman beat Ancell about the head with a stout club stick, knocking him to the ground. Ancell then, recovering his senses, made off along the road where Twyman caught up with him again at the Drapers (hospital) and knocked Ancell down again. The poor man begged on his knees to be allowed to live and Twyman, agreeing to leave him alone, now shook Ancell's hand, then with the utmost evil, he instantly raised his club with his other hand and smashed in Ancell's skull. The boy said his Master then gave the club to him and ordered him to hit Ancell, which he did. Twyman then walked his horse two or three times over the man to assure his death. The boy did not know where his master had gone.

A reward of 20 Guineas was offered by declaration in the local newspapers for the whereabouts of Charles Twyman. This encouraged one person to divulge that Twyman was hidden in a house at Northdown Margate but when the property was searched it was found he had already fled. Twyman was never apprehended. Whether he was ever seen again by his family of course is unknown. He could possibly have joined a ship and disappeared into the Navy. Twyman left a Wife and five children unsupported and Ancell left a widow and eight children on the parish. One man dead, one man on the run for life and two women left in poverty with 13 hungry children.

Interesting snippet: Drapers Hospital (almshouse) near Margate, was founded in 1708 by Michael Yoakley on land once belonging to Drapers Farm. Michael Yoakley's criteria for being admitted as an inmate was that all applicants must be:

"No busy-body, nor proud idle person, nor waster, but careful and diligent as much as in them lieth, labouring with their own hands for a maintenance, being of good life and Godly conversation as becometh the truth and the Christian religion"

The charity still operates today as a private home for the elderly and successful applicants for the almshouses must fit Yoakley's original criteria - according to the Yoakley House website.

Sources: Hampshire Chronicle 24 April 1786: Derby Mercury 20 April 1786: Kentish Gazette 28 April 1786:

St Peters Village Nr Broadstairs

7.

The Murder of Thomasine Ward 1807

The village of St Peter's Thanet is now part of Broadstairs but in 1807 it was still separated from the town by a small strip of open countryside.

On the evening of 16th January 1807 Mrs Thomasine Ward, aged 60, was walking home to her chandlers shop in St Peter's village after visiting one of her married daughters in Broadstairs town. It was a dark winter's night, around 9pm, so not a wise decision to be going out alone on a dark country road, but it was only one mile and perhaps she had no choice having left her daughter's house later than she intended. When Thomasine hadn't arrived home by 10pm her husband, William Ward, began to get very worried and set out to look for his wife. A crescent moon gave a faint light and several friends and neighbours soon joined the search with lanterns. The party retraced Mrs Ward's journey, setting off back towards Broadstairs.

Just before midnight a Mr Stephen May, helping in the search, found Thomasine lying in a field about 60 yards off of St Peter's Road. She had been strangled to death and had a thin length of ribbon tied twice, tight, around her neck. The poor woman had suffered much violence and had obviously put up a valiant struggle, her clothes being torn from her and her body left exposed. By the light of lanterns there could be seen the foot marks in the mud where two people had struggled, Thomasine and her attacker.

St Peters Village Nr Broadstairs

The victim was flat on her back, her mouth was wide open and next to her lay a handkerchief soaked in saliva that suggested it had been thrust into her mouth at some point to muffle her screams. Thomasine's body was taken home and an inquest held the next day. Mr Frome, a surgeon at Broadstairs, came and examined the corpse and declared there were no injuries that could have caused death other than the ligature around the neck. Despite her clothing being ripped there was no evidence of sexual molestation. Death resulted from asphyxiation. Luckily a witness came forward, Mr Henry Blackman (some reports say Blackburn), a local carpenter, who knew Mrs Ward, and said he had passed her on St Peter's road sometime between 8.30 and 9pm. He had spoken to her and said he was going to Broadstairs, she replied that she also was going home, all seemed well with the lady. He then passed a soldier in the uniform of the German Legion coming from Broadstairs, but saw no one else.

The Country Road to St Peter's where Thomasine Ward was Murdered

The German Legion were stationed nearby and enquiries were quickly made as to the whereabouts of all the soldiers on the night in question. (The KGL was a British Army unit of mostly German expats fighting against the French in the Napoleonic Wars. The 7th Battalion was based at Ramsgate but they also had a garrison in Broadstairs.) Sergeant Frederick Riford of the Legion informed the constables that only one soldier could not be accounted for as he had been absent without leave from his guard duty between 7 and 10pm, his name was Andreas Schestock. The soldier was Hungarian and spoke no English but could speak German well and so an interpreter was provided. Permission was then granted for his possessions to be searched. Two ladies handkerchiefs were found in his locker and another tucked inside his uniform cap. These hankies were the same as the one found by the murdered woman's body and later identified by William Ward as having belonged to his wife.

19th century illustration of a woman being murdered with a double wrapped cord

(Handkerchiefs were expensive prized possessions in those days and often embroidered with the owners initials)

Schestock claimed he had bunked off guard duty to go for a drink at the Neptune Hall tavern in Harbour Street Broadstairs and had later, on his home journey, seen a man knock down a woman and drag her into a field. The unknown man then came over and gave him the hankies. Probably the most lame story ever translated from German into English and the constables didn't believe a word of it plus Schestock hadn't even bothered to clean his boots which were still caked in thick field mud. Schestock was arrested for Thomasine's murder.

On Thursday March 26th Andreas Schestock stood trial at Maidstone Assizes and was found guilty. He was sentenced to be hanged and his body given up to surgeons at Maidstone hospital for dissection. After sentencing Schestock is reported to have said in German, "There is one God and one heaven, I pray for mercy." The Judge replied "Don't expect any in this world – take him away."

Schestock was given a German bible in Maidstone prison so he could make his prayers and confess his sins. A priest and an interpreter attended him. Andreas never confessed and stuck to his story of seeing a stranger murder the woman and receiving the three hankies as a gift from him.

The execution took place on Penenden Heath two days later on Saturday 28 March 1807.

Thomasine Ward had raised five children, worked hard all her life and had been murdered for just three hankies and the thrills of an evil psychopath.

Family Research: Thomasine Ward nee Morris was born 1747 at St Peter's village Thanet. Her parents were John Morris & Susannah Gray.

She married first Philip Jarman at St Peter's Church in 1771, they had 5 children; Susannah 1772, Thomas 1776, Ann 1778, John 1779 & Frances

1780. After her husband Philip Jarman died she married second husband William Ward 21 Oct 1787 at St Peter's. William & Thomasine do not appear to have had any children, together. They ran a chandlers shop in St Peter's village.

Sources: The British Newspaper Archives & Ancestry.com

8.

The Bizarre Death of Eleanor Tritton 1821

On 25th November 1821, Mr John Curling Esq the owner of Ozengell Grange, sited midway between Manston and St. Lawrence Ramsgate, gave his cook Eleanor Tritton, aged 26, permission to go visit her sister in Sandwich.

It was agreed that two of her fellow male servants should meet her on Haine road in the evening to escort her home in the dark at 9pm. The men, named John Castle and John Mummery, waited at the side of the road at the appointed time were they expected to meet Eleanor. A horse and gig approached in the dark where upon Castle called out "For Ozengell?" In reply, Eleanor, recognising Castle's voice, stood up and waved her arms screaming "Castle. For God's sake take me out of here " whereupon the driver pulled her back down into her seat and immediately whipped his horse to go faster, racing on down the road. Castle pursued the gig running as fast as he could. The gig turned from the Sandwich road onto the Canterbury road where John Castle observed Eleanor trying to jump from the gig, she called out "Lord have mercy upon us. Come on Castle." The gig then turned towards Chilton where Castle lost sight of it. John Castle then proceeded on to Ramsgate to see if the gig was in town. Eventually Castle spotted the gig coming out of the barracks and once again set off in pursuit following it up Broad Street, the High Street, Chatham street and finally onto the Margate road whereupon the driver whipped the horse harder and John Castle lost sight of it again. John Castle then returned home exhausted. By then it was 2am. He told John Mummery what had happened but as their master was asleep they dared not wake him until 5am to inform him. In the meantime the two men took a lantern and went out again together but did not find Eleanor.

When it was light, and the Master of Ozengell, Mr Curling, was awoken he was informed of events. Immediately he took his horse and set out to make inquiries. Eleanor's body was eventually discovered by an old gent collecting firewood, she was lying in a ditch at the side of the road, not miles away in Ramsgate but near the very spot where she was supposed to have alighted originally. Very peculiar. Enquiries were made in the vicinity as to who owned such a gig as described by Castle and it was soon established that it belonged to the Bull and George Inn at Ramsgate. The landlord confirmed that he had sent his post boy, John Payne, to drive a gentleman home to Sandwich on the night in question. John Payne was taken into custody accused of murdering Eleanor Tritton. At the inquest at Ramsgate. John Castle and John Mummery gave their evidence as did Mr John Curling. John Tipper the landlord of the Red Lion Inn at Stonar near Sandwich also gave evidence that John Payne had called at his Inn on the evening in question at around 9pm for a glass of gin. John Payne mentioned that he had offered a young woman a ride on the road a few minutes earlier but she had refused him. The landlord, concerned that a girl was walking alone in the dark. went outside and found Eleanor who asked him if there was anyone inside the Inn waiting for her from Ozengell, when he replied in the negative Eleanor insisted on walking on. John Payne then left in the gig heading in the same direction as the girl. John Payne himself refused to give any explanation of his actions that night.

(A bit confusing there being 5 men named John in this case)

Three doctors gave evidence that the deceased girl had small facial bruises consistent with a fall, and could have fallen on her face and suffocated in the mud after being knocked out from a fall. The deceased girl's Father insisted his daughter had been murdered and the Judge too, being dissatisfied with this explanation of death. ordered Eleanor's body to be exhumed and examined by more senior medical surgeons. Much to his own distress the girl's father insisted on being present throughout the autopsy and was accompanied, and supported in his distress, by John Curling, the girl's employer. The expert surgeons Messrs Giraud and Chambers came to much the same conclusion as the previous doctors, a bruise on the nose and a mouth filled with dried blood pointed to the deceased having suffered a burst blood vessel rendering her unconscious which resulted in suffocation due to the face downward fall into the dirt. The lungs also showed signs of suffocation. The girl had not been sexually molested.

John Payne was committed to Maidstone gaol to await trial at the next Assizes in March 1822 but only on the charge of manslaughter, the jury not being presented with any evidence that Payne had intentionally murdered the young woman.

On 30th March 1822 The jury at Maidstone found John Payne guilty of manslaughter and he was sentenced to pay a fine of 21 shillings and be imprisoned for one month in the county jail at Maidstone.

John Payne never explained why he had prevented Eleanor from leaving the gig and why he had taken her on a breakneck excursion in a circular route only for her to end up being found dead back near her home. One can only conclude that John Payne was legally advised by his defence to keep his silence and not incriminate himself as there were no witnesses or medical evidence to support him being guilty of causing Eleanor's death.

Eleanor Tritton was born 1795. Died 25 Nov 1821 aged 26. She was buried 2 Dec 1821 at All Saints Church Waldershare nr Dover where her family resided. Eleanor Tritton was very much liked by her master and his family and valued as a respectable hard working woman having been in the Curling's employment for over five years.

Source: Evening Mail 03 December 1821: Belfast Commercial Chronicle 30 March 1822: Kentish Weekly Post or Canterbury Journal - Friday 30 November 1821: Plus Ancestry.com

Ozengell Grange, not to be confuse with Ozengall farm opposite, the former home of Westler Jackie Pallo, The Grange itself is a grade 11 listed house on Haine Road Ramsgate. Both buildings are in derelict state.

9.

Strangled Baby on Ramsgate Beach 1863

At 9am on a November morning in 1863, Henry Pilcher was carting barrows of seaweed off of the beach at the the Royal crescent Ramsgate for his employer Mr Maxted. When he tipped out a barrow load of weed there was a large lump in it. Untangling the seaweed he found a new born baby, naked, with a knotted rag around its neck. The baby was wrapped up and handed to a work lad to convey to the local police station.

Mr H Milson the duty surgeon observed the child's umbilical cord was untied suggesting the infant had not been born in the presence of any medical person. When the rag was removed from the throat it was found to have been covering a large cut that had severed the windpipe back to the spine. Water in the lungs showed the baby must have been killed whilst under the sea or possibly in a bathtub (guess no one thought to test if it was salt water or not. I suggest bathtub or why would the wound be covered up with a cloth if it was killed where it was found, it wouldn't matter if it bled in the sea.) The child was judged to have been in the sea approximately 24 hours. An inquest found the unknown child was murdered by person or persons unknown.

Source: Kentish Chronicle 21 Nov 1863

ERNEST SOUTHEY ALIAS STEPHEN FORWOOD

10.

The Ramsgate Serial killer 1865

In 1865 A tall gentleman with a black beard, moustache and bushy side whiskers booked into the Camden Arms hotel in Ramsgate. He signed in as Ernest Southey. Next morning he asked a young porter, named William Tattenden, to run an errand. 17 year old Willy was to nip along to 38 Kings Street (on 1861 census) There he would find the home and workshop of Mr William Ellis, a stainer and dyer, and enquire of Mr Ellis if he might kindly furnish the address of one of his tenants, a Mrs Mary-Ann Forwood, and if so, then Willy was to deliver to the lady a note into her own hand. Willy did as asked and Mr Ellis directed him further up the street to number 93 Kings Street where his tenant, Mrs Mary-Ann Forwood was living (with her mother Jemima on 1861 census) There, Mrs Forwood gave the lad a note by return, in which she informed the gentleman that he might call on her. Later that day when Southey called on the lady he was refused admittance and kept on the doorstep. He then suggested Mrs Forwood might step outside and take a walk with him. Again his request was refused, Mrs Forwood had no wish to be seen out walking with a man that her neighbours would consider a stranger.

Camden Arms, La Belle Alliance Square, Ramsgate.

14 years earlier, Mary-Ann Jemima Draper had married a baker's assistant named Stephen Forwood. They had moved to Hastings in Sussex and there they were married. On signing the marriage registry in Hastings Stephen had added the name Southey as an addition to his surname, thus becoming Stephen Forwood Southey. The wife might not have noticed him

signing the register as such and the couple remained known as just Forwood. The couple then, reputedly, had a baby son whom they named Henry and were set to have a very comfortable life. Soon it became apparent that the marriage was not going to be a happy one after all. Forward hated being a baker, a profession he had reluctantly been apprenticed to as a youth. Mary-Ann's father, Benjamin Draper, a flour miller, financed Stephen in setting up in his own bakery, to be his own boss.

Stephen had an addiction to gambling. It wasn't long before he had gambled the business profits away and was deep in debt. Like all gamblers, Stephen's solution to his debts was to borrow more money to gamble with. Come 1857, and fearing arrest and debtors' prison, Stephen Forwood packed his bags and vanished into the night.

Over the next eight years Mary-Ann Forwood received a couple of anonymous letters containing the odd few shillings but no return address. At some time during this period it seems the child Henry died and Stephen Forwood could not be informed as his whereabouts were unknown.

Jump forward to 1865 and Stephen was on his wife's doorstep calling himself Ernest Walter Southey. He seemed like a stranger to her, he even looked completely different. Mary-Ann had no desire to be alone with this man but she agreed that there were matters to discuss, financial matters, but would prefer this to take place in the presence of her friends. Forwood reluctantly agreed. Mary-Ann told him to call at Mr Ellis' home in an hour.

William Ellis was Mrs Forwood's landlord, he was in his sixties, a widower. One of his three adult daughters kept house for him. Her name was Adelaide Ellis. She was 34 and a dressmaker the same as Mary-Ann Forwood. The two ladies being of the same occupation and similar age, Mary-Ann Forwood 36, they had become very close companions and confidants. Forwood was invited into the Ellis' parlour. Adelaide served tea. Mr Ellis struck up pleasant conversation with Forwood and then Mary-Ann introduced the pretty little girl in the room. "This is Emily, your daughter." she announced flatly. "And even though you have not concerned yourself as to ask after our son's health I tell you now that our lad died". Forwood showed no emotion to the news of his own son's death but outwardly feigned surprise and delight at the revelation of a daughter whilst inwardly he was dejected. He had no idea his wife had been pregnant again when he had left her, but the child was 8 years old and had a family resemblance and so he kissed the girl on the forehead and resumed conversation with the party. Forwood recounted tales of his travels around England and how life had dealt him incredible blows and misfortune. No matter how hard he had tried to raise his station in life, to his rightful place amongst his peers, others, through no fault of his own, had always conspired to knock him back down the social ladder, indeed, he had once a fortune of £1,700 that had been cruelly swindled from him. He talked of playing billiards and gaming with Lord Dudley and of communications with the Earl of Shaftesbury amongst other worthy persons he considered his intellectual equal. He even appeared to be on personal acquaintance with the Prime Minister and the Archbishop of Canterbury! Forwood was full of his own grandeur and talked only of himself; he showed no interest in enquiring of the life of his wife and daughter.

Mary-Ann was getting annoyed, here this arrogant man sat, taking of enormous sums he had gained and lost whilst she had struggled to raise their child alone in desperate poverty working all hours God sent. Who the devil did he think he was. He was a smuggler's brat, a lowly bread seller, a nothing-monger who had sneaked off in the night leaving her to face his creditors, and now he put on airs and graces and talked of his 'rightful place' amongst the upper classes. Mary wasn't going to listen to this rubbish any longer. Where was her money, where was the eight years maintenance that he owed for little Emily and herself, where was the money she had paid his creditors? Forwood expressed his desire to communicate with his wife in private. Mary-Ann refused.

Mr Ellis was not impressed with Forwood either. The atmosphere became explosive. Mr Ellis suggested that maybe all parties should calm themselves, leave, and meet again the next day if deemed really necessary. Forwood reluctantly left stating he did have further matters to communicate with his wife and desired to see his child again. Ellis agreed he could return at 8.30am the next morning.

Stephen Forwood had a poor start in life. Born in St Lawrence Ramsgate in 1829, his father, William Forwood, had reputedly been a smuggler, as had most of the male population of Thanet at one time or another. Already elderly at the time of Stephen's birth, with a prior marriage having produced grown children, William Forwood had died when his son Stephen was 3 years old. Sarah, Stephen's mother, worked as a washerwoman and struggled to raise him and his three young siblings. When she died c1842, Stephen was 13 and apprenticed to a local baker named Gore. An older half-brother acted as his guardian.

In 1851, aged 22, Stephen was living with a baker named Attwood-Lacey in Ramsgate but left later that year to marry his sweetheart Miss Mary-Ann Jemima Draper. Stephen and Mary-Ann were married in Hastings and that is where Stephen signed the register as Forwood-Southey. (Why he had given himself this added surname is a mystery but in hindsight he was obviously taking his first step to a change of identity.) Forwood then set up as a baker on his own account. It seemed Forwood's life was all planned out for him now - but oh, how he began to loath it. The baker's lad was a dreamer. Only educated at the penny-a-week village school, he was surprisingly intelligent. He read the classics and poetry and aspired to a literary life, debating politics and philosophy with men he considered his intellectual equal. It may be that his name change was in homage to popular author and poet at the time, Robert Southey. Forwood wanted more out of life than making and selling bread rolls. Soon he was living beyond his means and the bakery failed with debts. Stephen had an insatiable taste for gambling. Naturally, this only made his situation worse. He was a failure as a baker and an even worse failure as a gambler.

Initially after he decamped, Forwood wandered aimlessly around Britain from Scotland to the Isle of Wight and even across to Ireland. He was a failure at everything he tried his hand at, always running away to escape creditors.

In 1861 he found himself in Brighton on the Sussex coast. He gained employment in a billiard hall as a chalker (marking the game scores.) There he learned to play the game himself and soon found he was very good at it and could earn extra money playing for bets.

At number 7, St. Georges Terrace Brighton, a Mrs Maria Ann White had opened up her home as a dame school. The lady had recently come from Holborn in London where she had separated from her husband, who was also a teacher. She had four small children to support by herself. Teaching from home was not her idea of fun but needs must, and she found several pupils that were willing to board. In the 1861 census she had four boarding pupils, a servant and a nursemaid. One day on the seafront she made the acquaintance of Stephen Forwood, now calling himself Ernest

Walter Southey. Stephen was instantly smitten. Before long he had promised to take care of Maria and her four children and so moved into her house. The couple become lovers. The school could obviously not continue under this shameful set up. The pupils left and the school closed. Once again Forwood had lumbered himself with the burden of domesticity.

One evening, a chance game of billiards triggered the start of events that would drive Stephen's life from that point on.

The Honourable Humble Dudley-Ward (1821-1870) was in the club playing billiards. He offered to play Stephen for a five shilling bet. Thinking he would win easily and Stephen would not be able to afford the loss, Dudley-Ward announced that all debts must be settled before leaving the club. Stephen agreed and won. Dudley-Ward was incredulous, the gutter snipe must have cheated. He challenged Stephen to play again, increasing the stakes. Stephen won again. Dudley-Ward now owed him £122 and knew he couldn't pay up, so like all gamblers do, he challenged Stephen again, upping the stakes with ridiculous odds. Stephen won fair and square and now demanded his winnings. A whopping £1,720. Not surprisingly Dudley-Ward didn't have this amount of money about him, so he hastily left saying he would pay later that month. Naively Stephen took the 'honourable' gent at his word and went home that night on cloud nine. Truth unbeknown to Stephen, Dudley-Ward was broke and had gambling debts all over the country.

Maria and Stephen celebrated. This was their big chance. They could do all the things they had dreamed of. Stephen called on Ward several times to collect his winnings. Each time he could not get past the servants who, to add insult, also gave him the boot. Maria then attempted to collect the money herself. She was thrown off the premises and tried to report Humble

Dudley-Ward for assault. No-one believed her and she had no money for a private action. The couple became obsessed with getting the money they considered was legally owed to then. They stalked Dudley-Ward and begged his relatives to intervene. They were ignored. Stephen lost his job over it and with Maria not working either, they soon found themselves homeless. Reduced to begging and dragging the four children from one dirty lodging house to the next they descended into a kind of obsessive madness. Their days became consumed with writing letters to every prominent personage imaginable. The Archbishop of Canterbury. Lord Shaftesbury, Gladstone, Disraeli, all received letters informing them of the terrible injustice that Stephen and his family had suffered because of the Hon. Dudley-Ward. Most begging letters were simply ignored, others were actually answered, the receivers stating it was not their concern. A few had sympathy with Stephen and enclosed a few shillings and even the odd gold sovereign for the children.

Eventually Maria had the good sense to realise this state of affairs could not continue. One day, when Stephen was out, Maria packed her things, took her four children and disappeared.

Now Stephen had a new obsession, finding Maria.

On August 5th 1865, Forwood found out that Maria had left the children with a child minder in Battersea by the name of Sarah Petty. She lived at 2 Cornelia Terrace. He wrote a letter immediately, informing Maria that if she did not return to him then something terrible would happen that she could never imagine. Forwood then went straight to Battersea intending to leave the letter with the childminder.

Mrs Petty had never seen Forwood before, but she had been warned about him, so when he insisted he was the children's father and demanded to see them, Mrs Petty knew he was lying and refused him entrance. She said only the girl, Eliza Annie, was staying with her, the boys were with their real father. Forwood gave Sarah the letter intended for Maria and Sarah told Forwood that she wouldn't be able to give Maria the letter for a long time as Mrs White was already on her way to Australia. She had left little Eliza Annie with Sarah on July 20th and taken passage on a ship from Liverpool on the 24th. Once she had arranged for their new life in Australia she would be sending for her children. Stephen exploded, shoving Sarah aside he tried to snatch the little girl. The child was terrified, she seemed to hate Stephen, she screamed and ran away. Mrs petty threatened to scream for the police herself and so Stephen ran away.

Stephen could not believe what had happened. How could Maria have gone off to Australia when all he had ever done was care for her and her children. Maria would pay for this disloyalty, he would make her suffer. He knew where Maria's estranged husband, William Stallwood White, lived at Featherstone Buildings in Holborn. Mr White knew that Southey was his wife's lover, but had no time for him. Stephen put on his best behaviour like a cheap suit and went to see one of White's grown up sons, by a prior marriage, Josiah White. He too lived in Holborn and knew Forwood-Southey as his step mother's lover. Stephen said, lying, that he had missed the boys and was going to join Maria, who had requested he collect her boys from their father and bring them with him. Forwood explained that he thought a difficulty might arise with Mr White as they did not get along. Therefore he wondered if perhaps Josiah might intermediate and collect the boys for him? Josiah said he would try. And true to his word the next day he brought his three half-brothers to Stephen. Forwood told the boys of all the fun and treats they should have and William, Thomas and little

Alexander agreed to go off with him thinking they were going to meet their Mother.

William Stallwood White was a school teacher in Holborn and appears to have been a poor Father and an emotionally weak man. He had been a widower when he married Maria and already had seven children, most grown up, and none of whom were currently living with him. He had obviously not been warned about Stephen and Maria having split up, or Maria's intention to go abroad. Maria had dropped the three boys off saying it was only for the weekend. Mr White and Josiah now also assumed the boys were happily on their way back to their loving Mother. They were not. After plying the boys with cakes and lemonade Stephen only took them a distance of a few streets to Starr's coffee house in Red Lion Street Holborn. There he asked if the three boys could have a bed for two nights. This agreed, Stephen settled them in bed before leaving, saying he had work to attend to. Next day he returned saying the travel arrangements were delayed but they would be off the next day. That evening he again settled the boys for the night telling the staff he had business to attend to and would collect the boys first thing in the morning to begin their journey home to their Mother.

He never returned. It was a maid who found the three boys the next day. She had gone to wake them and see what they wanted for breakfast. All three were still neatly tucked in their beds, stone cold dead. A substance that had oozed from their mouths was dried on their tortured little faces. A bottle of prussic acid was on a table.

A major hunt was now launched to find the monstrous fiend, the slayer of the three innocent children. But where to look, who were these children?

The outrage quickly became the only talk in London. Hearing the news, and fearing from the description given in the newspapers that the three anonymous boys might be his sons, William Stallwood White was faced with the horrendous task of identifying the three little bodies. Now the hunt was on for Ernest Walter Southey, the 'Monster of Holborn'.

Dr George Harley who conducted the autopsy on the three murdered boys

Meanwhile, down in Ramsgate, Mary-Ann Forwood and little Emily were having breakfast with Adelaide and William Ellis. Stephen Forwood showed up at 8.20am, he was an eager ten minutes early. Adelaide gave him a dish of tea and Mr Ellis went into his workshop to begin his daily labour. Twice Stephen asked that he might be allowed to speak to his wife in private. Eventually Mary-Ann relented and Adelaide said they might go upstairs to her private sitting room if they wished while Emily could stay downstairs and help her with the dishes. After a few minutes, Forwood called down for little Emily to come up and join her parents. Adelaide was in the kitchen when she heard two gunshots. Alarmed, she ran to the foot of the stairs in time to hear a third shot and see little Emily fall to the landing floor. The child began to roll down the stairs as Adelaide rushed up the steps to catch her. Stephen was now at the top of the stairs and pointed a gun at Adelaide. Bravely she held onto Emily and screamed for her father. William Ellis rushing in. Showing no fear he ran up the stairs and tackled Stephen, grappling the gun from his hand. Forwood sank down onto a chair. He did not try to fight Ellis. Only then did Mr Ellis see a pair of legs protruding from behind a table. Mary-Ann Forwood lay dead.

William Ellis was amazed. Forwood now looked completely different. "What have you done?" yelled Ellis "and..and..where is your beard?"

Stephen removed his hairy disguise from his pocket and handed it over saying " You go fetch the police, yes you do that." Ellis now held Forwood under arrest until the police could get there. Adelaide ran off to fetch them, her generous heart sending her first for a surgeon to help little Emily. When two surgeons, Hicks and Curling, arrived it was already too late, Emily was as dead as her Mother. Both had been shot in the head at close range. Stephen Forwood was arrested and went quietly.

At Ramsgate police station the coppers were scratching their heads. Forwood was insisting his name was Ernest Walter Southey, whilst an older policeman was swearing he knew that pompous voice anywhere, it was Stephen Forwood who was once a baker's boy local to Ramsgate. Forwood agreed the woman and child were his but denied murdering them. Indeed, he was totally innocent. He had only done them a favour, they would no longer be dependent on him and were better off dead. Forwood then launched into a long boring speech on the woes of social injustice and how events had conspired against him until he was dragged down into poverty and was emotionally drained bla bla bla. As the police yawned, and no doubt rolled their eyes, Stephen blamed Dudley-Ward, the Archbishop of Canterbury, the Prime Minister and everyone but himself for the misfortune that had befallen him. Then, just as the police were convinced they really must have an escaped lunatic on their hands, Forwood asked if they had not heard of the Holborn murders? The Ramsgate cops said they had heard something, but what had that to do with him? Forwood seemed pleased to inform them that he had recently poisoned three small children in Holborn and that, if they were to enquire there, they might find that the Metropolitan police were searching for him.

From then on policemen flew in all directions. Bobbys were sent to London and coppers came down to Ramsgate. The town's folk had never heard anything like it. The Kings Street killer was also the Monster of Holborn and now he was caught, locked up and ranting like a loon in Ramsgate cage.

It was quickly decided that a secure prison was needed to hold a criminal of Forwood's calibre. Stephen was chained up in a closed fly (horse drawn coach) and whisked away to be secured in manacles at Sandwich goal.

The inquest on the Holborn children, William, Thomas and Alexander White, had already been held at the Queen Arms in Red lion Passage on Aug 17th, 1865. Their Mother, Mrs White, could not be found, she was presumably still on her way to Australia. Mrs Petty gave evidence as did Mr White, his son Josiah White and the staff at the coffee house. A chemist named Bloxhall said Forwood/Southey had previously enquired of him the price of Prussic acid, but had not purchased it from him.

The verdict was wilful murder of the three children by Forwood/Southey who was still at large at that time.

The inquest into the deaths of Mary-Ann Forwood & Emily Forwood was held at Ramsgate Town Hall, it was very protracted as Stephen insisted on being present in court to proclaim his innocence thus:

"I could bear the struggle no longer, my sufferings were no longer supportable. The last hope had perished by my bitter and painful experience of our present iniquitous, defective social justice system. I am charged with criminal murder in the truest and strongest sense. I deny and repudiate that charge, and throw it back on the men who have by their gross criminal neglect so brought about this fearful crime by turning a deaf ear on my heartbroken appeals." Stephen then ranted on for ages on the unfairness of his lot. He scribbled notes and handed out letters that he wanted delivered and insisted it was all Dudley-Ward's fault. The court and the public in the packed gallery were fascinated but equally convinced Stephen Forwood was a raving lunatic.

The verdict was wilful murder by Ernest Southey alias Stephen Forwood. The coroner ordered he be examined by medical professionals as to whether he was insane or not before he was committed to trial.

The borough of Holborn demanded Stephen be tried there for the murder of the three White boys. Maidstone assizes insisted he be tried first at Maidstone for Mary-Ann and Emily's murders as he was already under their jurisdiction.

Forwood was moved to Maidstone gaol until his trial was held in Maidstone Court house. As you can imagine it lasted for an entire day. Stephen again ranted and gave speeches. Dozens of witnesses had to be called from London, Sussex and Kent to provide evidence. Forwood objected to everything and everyone including the jury and even his own defence council. Then he stopped proceedings again to object to the new camera that had been set up in the court.

"Why should he, an innocent man, have his likeness taken."

The camera then had to be removed.

Forwood maintained his claim that his wife and daughter and Maria's four children had all been wholly dependant on him and so he had released them, (except the girl Annie who had escaped) from their misery by sending them to a better place (heaven) This was seen as an outrageous claim by the eyes of the courthouse. The three boys had been safe with their real father and Mrs White had already broken off with Stephen. The boys were no longer Forwood's responsibility or his concern. His wife and daughter in Ramsgate had not seen him for eight years and had established an independent life of their own which Forwood was not financially contributing to. It was plain to everyone that Forwood had killed 5 people out of pure malicious spite, especially in the case of the three boys. But he was not being tried for the death of the boys at Maidstone, only for the Ramsgate murders. If found not guilty he would then be moved to Holborn and tried there for that outrage on the boys.

The Maidstone jury had no doubts at all in finding Forwood/Southey guilty of murder with wilful intent. They were only unsure as to whether or not he was insane.

Experts from several asylums had examined Stephen in prison. Two doctors did consider him mad, but others insisted he was perfectly sane, arguing that he had deliberately disguised himself, purchased a revolver, and taken it with him for the sole intent of murdering his wife and daughter and had intentionally plotted his crime. The death sentence was then handed down and the crowd applauded vigorously.

Outside an enormous crowd now bayed for Forwood/Southey's blood. They would have preferred an old school public lynching there and then. Hurriedly the police bundled Stephen out the back of the court and rushed him off back to Maidstone gaol.

Forwood spent his last days feverishly writing letters, over 200 of them, and boring the pants off fellow prisoners with his long speeches on social injustice. Finally he asked for a letter to be delivered to the Hon. Humble Dudley-Ward stating that he forgave him. There were also letters for Mrs white should she ever return from Australia.

Ernest Walter Southey alias Stephen Forwood was executed on Thursday 11th Jan 1866 at 12 noon outside Maidstone gaol by William Calcraft assisted by Mr Smith. He protested his innocence to the last. The weather was exceptionally foul, a biting east wind brought heavy falls of snow, the crowd was therefore smaller than expected, less than 500 and barely a woman amongst them. He suffered little on the short drop barely twitching. A plaster death mask was then cast of his face and he was then buried in the prison yard.

Forwood had always courted public attention and now he had it. His wax likeness was for many years displayed in the chamber of horrors at Madame Tussauds.

Family records:

Stephen's surname was variously, and still is, reported as being spelt Forward. It was definitely Forwood as attested to by registration, census and the court records.

Stephen Forwood was baptised Aug 1829 St Lawrence, Ramsgate. His Parents were William Forwood & Sarah Mears.

His Father: William Forwood died 1832 St Lawrence, Ramsgate when Stephen was 3yrs old. His Mother Sarah, a charwoman, died in 1842 when Stephen was 13 yrs old. He had many siblings.

Mary-Ann Jemima Draper born 1st July 1828 Margate, baptised as an adult 25 June 1843 and gave her address as 14 East Road Margate. Her parents were Benjamin Draper (born Margate 1804) & Jemima Ram Bone (1801-1885) They married 4 May 1824 Margate. Benjamin Draper was a relation of the owners named Draper, of the three Margate Windmills site known as Drapers mill, Little Drapers Mill and the pumper mill. The largest, Drapers Mill, was replaced by a new mill in 1845 by a John Holman of Canterbury but retained the Draper name; the windmill at Rye was also originally named Drapers Mill. The Drapers were a large family in 18thc Thanet with several roads and farms named after them. It would make sense that a baker's boy and a mill worker's daughter should get to meet each other.

Mary-Ann Jemima Draper Married Stephen Forward-Southey 1851 Hastings Sussex

Their daughter Emily Sarah Frances Forwood was baptised 1857 St Lawrence, Ramsgate. As for the baby son named Henry, I was unable to find evidence for his baptism or burial.

Coincidently, there was another Stephen Forwood living in Ramsgate with a wife also called Mary-Ann at the same time. He lived until the 1890s, was a cooper (barrel maker) and had several sons which may account for the errors in many old re-tellings of this case.

After the murder of Mary-Ann and little Emily the Mother, Jemima Ram Draper nee Bone, already widowed by the time of her daughter's death, moved to Battle in Sussex to board with relatives and then later to Islington London where she died in 1885 aged 84 having outlived her entire family, poor lady must have had a sad old age.

Maria White was born Maria Milner 16 Sept 1832 St Paul's London daughter of Henry Milner. She married William Stallwood White at St Pancras London in 1853. There is no record of Maria White or/Milner/Forwood/Southey ever having gone to Australia. So was this just a cover story to dodge the lunatic Forwood? I doubt it or she would have appeared at the boys funerals and the court case. I suspect she just used an Alias name to travel. It is unknown what became of her after the murder of her sons. Her daughter Eliza Annie White also vanished from records. It seems most likely Mother and daughter united and changed their names to avoid publicity. Some sources claim the 4 children of Maria White were fathered by Stephen, this is not true. The children were all born before Maria met Stephen and baptised in Holborn between 1855 and 1858 by their Father William Stallwood White. (1807-1892) William Stallwood

White was Previously married to Ann Turner by whom he had already fathered about 8 children.

Locations:

The Star Coffee House was 21 Red Lion Street Holborn and has long since been demolished.

38 Kings Street Ramsgate where the wife and daughter were murdered seems to have been replaced by an Edwardian row of shops c1900.

Sources: Dover express 19 Aug 1865. Cambridge Chronicle and Journal 13 January 1866. Norwich mercury 12 Aug 1865. Kentish Gazette 16 January 1866. Dublin Evening Mail 31 August 1865. Sheffield Daily Telegraph 6 August 1865. A further large assortment of other newspapers articles plus internet searches and blogs. Family research through Ancestry.com.

11.

Murder by Salmestone Grange 1876

Shortly after 9am, the black flag was run up above Maidstone prison. It was April 4th 1876. State executioner William Marwood had performed his task. Mary Bridger's killer was officially dead.

Since the law had been changed in 1868, against the general wishes of the greater public, executions had since that time been performed in private, within the walls of England's prisons. Consequently, there was no gallows crowd and few bothered to wait outside in the rain for the hoisting of the flag although the family of the killer's victim probably did to bring them closure.

Like most Mary-Anns. Mary Bridger was always known as Polly. She was not what my Mother would have called, a decent young lady, for more often than not her behaviour was thoroughly indecent. Polly liked a drink. In fact Polly liked more than A drink, she liked to get totally bladdered and make a public spectacle of herself in the pubs around Margate. She was not alone in her choice of relaxation, she was usually accompanied by her man friend - A local widowed man of 48, with whom she had been going about for a long time.

Anyone who knew Tommy Fordred, also knew Polly Bridger, they were always out drinking and their regular weekend pub crawls always ended up the same way - Get totally drunk, shout and be rowdy, then stagger up to Salmestone chapel, where Fordred had been dossing, and spend the night there together.

Since losing his wife, Tommy had been doing casual labour at Salmestone Grange. Tom had been living rent free dossing down in the old deconsecrated chapel, then used as a hay barn.

On the 8th of January, Polly said 'see ya later' to her mum and went out. She was 33 years old and hoping for a fun evening. After working all week as a charwoman, Saturday night was party night. Polly wanted to let her hair down.

It was just after 5pm. Polly was dressed in poor but clean clothes and her mum thought she looked lovely. Tommy had arranged to meet Polly in a local pub. Once there they had several drinks and then moved on to the next pub. Just after 7.30pm, they moved along to the Liverpool Arms in Charlotte Place Margate and there they had more drinks. Polly's parents popped in and had a few drinks with them. The Bridgers lived in Church Street, at 9 Woods cottages, a stone's throw from the pub. The Bridgers disliked Tommy Fordred but as they had no say in their grown up daughter's relationship they accepted him as her choice of boyfriend, despite him often hitting her.

That evening Tom was noted to be in a mood. He called Polly a bitch a few times in front of witnesses and also gave her a slap and warned her about going out with other men. But all this was par for the course between Pol and Tom.

After a few more tots of rum, Tommy told his fellow pub mates that he and Pol were 'off for a feed' meaning they were going off to buy something to eat. So off they went to Pain's stores in Victoria Road Margate and bought some provisions, then to Pamphlett the butchers for 3 lb of cooked Pork which the butcher provided in an earthenware dish. (Meat was very cheap in the past) The local constable, PC Bradley, later found the couple, intoxicated, rowdy and shouting in the street. Having a word with them, he told them to be quiet and get off home.

Liverpool Arms, Margate (author)

Thomas Fordred was well known to the Police, he was a habitual criminal and had been in prison several times for thieving. Fordred then hissed at the copper and said they were going home anyway. The PC escorted them to the parish boundary, which for St John's was the bottom of a hill known as the 'First and last.' There the officer left the couple.

Tom and Polly staggered on towards their destination, the old chapel at Salmestone Grange. On the road they were passed by a chap named William Brenchley driving a pony and cart. He noticed the couple were drunk and heard Thomas Fordred call Polly an "old bitch."

Further on, a woman waiting for a lift at Salmestone crossroads, later recalled being nervous as she heard a couple arguing and fighting behind the bushes. When the man shouted 'You old bitch, I'll do for you.' The woman, Mrs Mary Shoaff, became frightened and decided to move on. No more was seen or heard of Tom and Polly for the next couple of hours.

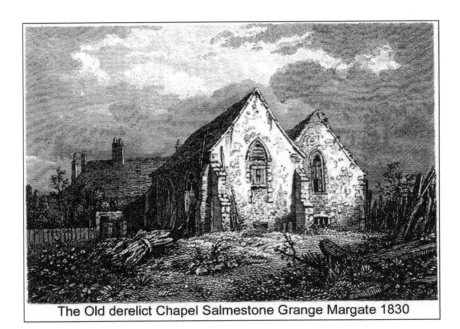
The Old derelict Chapel Salmestone Grange Margate 1830

George Emptage was a waggoner who lived at old Salmestone Grange farm with his family. Just after 10.30pm his wife got into bed. Mrs Emptage then heard her kitchen door open. Thinking it was her husband coming in, she went back downstairs. There was nobody there. By the back door she found a torn woman's blouse on the floor. She found her husband was still in the stables seeing to his horses. Just then Tom Fordred appeared in the stable, he was covered in scratches and blood. His clothes were blood stained too and he was obviously drunk, but not staggering or falling about.

George and Ann Emptage knew Tom and Polly, but not as friends, and they knew the pair often slept in the old chapel. Ann recognised the torn blouse as one Polly often wore. It was quite threadbare, old, and tore easily. When Fordred said to Emptage, "Come help me get Pol up to the barn, she's dead drunk and laying in the road" Mr Emptage didn't think it was that odd of a request. After all, Polly was often completely legless.

When Emptage saw the state of Polly lying in the road he must have rolled his eyes and shaken his head. She was stark naked but for her stockings and shoes. Tom said she was out cold and asked Emptage to get her up onto Tom's shoulders. Then Fordred carried Polly to the chapel and Emptage walked back with them, it was a short distance. Once at the chapel door, Emptage left them and went back to the stables to finish rubbing down his horses.

After Tom dropped Polly down in the hay he soon realised that something was wrong, Polly wasn't breathing. The young woman was not dead drunk, she was really dead.

There was no point in running, everyone had seen Fordred with Polly so Tommy covered Polly's body with hay and took himself off to the police station to report the matter and try to explain what had happened.

When the police removed Polly Bridger from the barn it was found she had severe wounds to the back of her head, marks and bruising from what appeared to be punches or foot marks and a lot of scratches, especially to the back of her hands which looked as if she had been dragged along the road backwards. They requested an immediate autopsy. The scene in the road near Salmestone Grange, where Mr Emptage had found the naked woman, showed clear evidence of a brutal struggle. Blood and drag marks extended over a full nine to ten yards from one side of the road to the other. Tufts of Polly's hair were also found, as were her torn skirt and under garments. The dish that had contained the pork was not just broken, it was smashed to smithereens. There was no pork I it. (Some lucky fox or rat had scored himself a 3 lb pork supper.) Thomas Fordred was arrested under suspicion of causing the death of Mary Ann Bridger. He was held in Margate police station until the inquest.

Fordred was brought to the inquest in his shirt sleeves, his blood stained jacket was kept as evidence. He was adamant that Polly had done it to herself. "The bitch kept falling over, " he explained. "I'd stand her up and then the bitch would fall down again." Fordred showed complete indifference to Polly's death. He frequently referred to her as "The bitch" and said she was falling over a lot and banging her own head on the stony road. She had striped herself off, he claimed, and he had just picked up her clothes for her, intending to take them to the chapel. He had left the blouse at the farm house whilst he looked for George Emptage. Polly Bridger's death was an accident, all her own doing. The autopsy results proved him a liar.

From the wounds on the back of the head, the deceased woman had obviously been hit with something. The wounds were too severe and deep to have been caused by falling in the road, also tufts of her hair having been pulled out was not commensurate with just falling down frequently. The palms of the hands were not grazed, as might be expected by one continuously falling and trying to get up again, but the backs of the hands were badly grazed and bloody suggesting the hands were limp and were dragged along the road. The collar bone showed severe bruising and marks indicative of much beating and probable kicking. The chest was the most damaged. This has undergone severe beating and showed evidence of marks suggesting foot prints and hob nail marks from a boot sole. The chest was crushed and this had caused internal injuries which in turn had been the cause of death.

The conclusion was Polly had been bashed over the head, badly kicked and beaten, swung about by her hair, punched and her clothes ripped from her. Finally her chest had been viciously stamped upon. She had also been dragged from one side of the road to the other. The jury decided Mary Bridger had been murdered by Thomas Fordred.

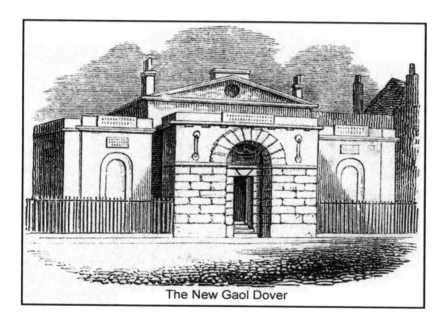

The New Gaol Dover

Maidstone Gaol where most Kent criminals were hanged from 1863

The crowd in the court were very angry. Thomas was swiftly marched away, and taken by train to Dover gaol to await trial for murder at the next Maidstone Assizes.

All Fordred was concerned about was whether or not he could have his pea green jacket back as it was freezing in Dover gaol, he knew that because he'd been in there before. He was refused the coat as it was evidence but a warder said he would find him some warm clothing.

At his trial, the public crowd was enormous. They exhibited a lot of anger and hostility towards the accused. Even so, Fordred stuck to his story. It was all Polly's own fault, the 'bitch' had done it to herself. Continuing to refer to the dead woman as "the bitch" and calling her "a bad lot" he showed total disrespect and not a glimmer of empathy for his deceased lover or her distraught family. This attitude won him no favours with the public nor jury. Accepting that there was no premeditation in the death of Mary Ann Bridger, the verdict was manslaughter. The sentence was still death. Had Thomas Fordred shown some empathy for the deceased, and remorse for being the cause of her death, the sentence might have been expected to then be commuted to life in prison or transportation. However, Thomas never showed any remorse except for the position he himself was in. Consequently no reprieve was granted and he was hanged at Maidstone Prison. Even on the gallows platform he maintained his innocence. His only crime, as he saw it, was allowing 'Pol' to get in that state.

Family Search:

Mary Ann Bridger born 1843 Margate. Daughter of John and Ann Bridger. She had many siblings.

Buried 12th Jan 1876 at St Johns the Baptist church Margate.

Thomas Fordred born 1828 Garlinge Margate.

Thomas' former wife Mary Paramour died 1863. Their 3 children were Jane, Fanny and Charles Fordred. The girls were teenagers and in service by the time their father died, the son had already been adopted soon after his mother's death in 1863 and changed his name to that of his adopted parents, Steed.

Thomas Fordred was hanged 4th April 1876 and was buried within the yard of Maidstone Prison in Kent.

Location: The old 14th century chapel at Salmestone Grange is no longer used as a barn. It has been restored and is now used for civil wedding ceremonies.

Sources: Whitstable Times and Herne Bay Herald - Saturday 22 January 1876. Thanet Advertiser 18 March 1876. Tamworth Herald 8 April 1876 Bedfordshire Mercury 1 April 1876. York Herald 4 April 1876 Dundee Courier April 1876. Ancestry.com

12.

The Baby down the Toilet 1878

James and Eliza Appleton lived in a row of five cottages at Hereson, a hamlet on the skirts of Ramsgate. The cottages were called Sackett's Cottages. They had lived there seven years, and shared, with the other residents, a privy (outside Lavatory) at the rear of the terrace.

James and his neighbours decided on the 19th March 1878 that it was time to dig out the waste from the vault under the privy. It had last been done four and a half years previous and it needed doing again. The rotted soil (composted excrement and newspaper and hay used as toilet paper) was usually then spread on the vegetable gardens as fertiliser. (It doesn't smell once it's well composted) Climbing down a ladder and digging the soil into buckets, Appleton jokingly called out to his workmates above "Look out, here comes a youngster" and threw up to them what he thought was a kid's rag doll. It wasn't. It was a real youngster. The half mummified remains of a baby much like a peat bog body. The corpse was placed in a shed and the police informed. Mr Griggs, police surgeon, examined the body, what remained of it, and estimated that as there were 20 tiny teeth it was approximately 16-18 months old when it died. The sex could not be determined nor the cause of death because of decomposition. PC Bradley took a sample of baby hair and washed it. It dried dark and was inclined to curl. He then made inquiries as to who had had access to the privy in the last year or so. The name of one previous tenant was brought up by several of the residents and PC Bradley went to find the young woman who was believed to be living in the Thanet Union workhouse. Clara Brockman was 23 and had been in the workhouse several times. In 1876 Clara had been admitted into the Thanet union heavily pregnant and destitute. She gave birth to a male child there on March 25. 1876. A birth certificate had been issued. The boy was registered in April 1876 as Sidney Harold Brockman, no father's name recorded. Shortly afterwards Clara and her child left the workhouse.

In May 1877 Clara got a job in a local laundry and needed someone to look after Sidney. Mrs Anne Siphert lived at 2 Rodney Street Ramsgate, she was a child minder and offered to care for Sidney for 5 shillings a week. The baby was then in good health, well fed and had light curly hair. After 3 weeks, and having only been paid for the first week, Mrs Silphert refused to mind Sidney anymore. Clara was then living in a house by the North Pole pub in Hereson Road. In June Clara moved into Sacketts cottages. The neighbours were very friendly and often invited Clara into their kitchens for tea and a chat. Maria Castle, Susannah Woodward and Elizabeth Appleton, the neighbours, all remembered baby Sidney well. Clara told the neighbours that she had an Aunt at Birchington who was willing to take Sidney and give him a good home. On 8 June 1877 she left with Sidney for her Aunt's house. Later that evening Clara returned with the boy and said her Aunt wasn't in but her father would take the boy the next morning. The next night Clara returned without Sidney but she had his clothes with her, saying that her Aunt didn't need the baby's old things, Clara sold the baby's clothes to Maria Castle for a few pennies. The clothes were a plaid frock, blue pelisse (jacket) and a black cap. (Victorian boys wore dresses until they went to school) Clara stayed a few more weeks and then told her neighbours that she'd had a letter saying Sidney was ill, she said she was going to visit him, later she claimed he was already dead when she got to her Aunt's house. The neighbours felt sorry for Clara and gave her a black shawl and decorated her hat with black crepe so she could attend Sidney's funeral. Shortly after this Clara moved out. (turns out she was already pregnant again) In January 1878 she was admitted to the Thanet workhouse yet again and birthed another child on the 8 Jan 1878 but she left before it could be registered so name and sex are unknown. The matron at the workhouse remembered Clara birthing Sidney back in 1876 and asked where the boy was. "Oh he died," replied Clara.

Clara was later admitted to the workhouse for the third time. When the police came to interview Clara two months after the body had been found the matron told the police about the births of Clara's two babies. PC Bradley now told Clara that the remains of a baby had been found at Sacketts Cottages and asked her where Sidney was. Clara told a completely different story from her previous accounts. She claimed her father had taken Sidney to a woman called Mrs Henry near Birchington, not an Aunt, and when she herself had gone there to visit no one had ever heard of Mrs Henry. She had never seen Sidney again and didn't know what had happened to him. The police checked the death register and found no entry for a death and interviewed Clara's father.

Thanet Union (Workhouse) built in 1836 postcard c1930

James Brockman was a miller's carter who worked at the windmill in Grange Road Ramsgate. He lived at Mill Cottages and was a married man who had 14 children of his own and was well respected locally. Mr Brockman had not seen his daughter Clara for a long time. He had heard through the local grapevine that she had had two children, but he had never seen anything of Clara for years; he had never seen her two children. He knew nothing of Clara's life, nor where she lived, and said Clara had no Aunt in or near Birchington. The police then arrested Clara for the wilful murder of little Sidney.

At Clara's trial on 13 July 1878, her father gave the same evidence and seemed very distressed at having to prove his daughter a liar. After giving evidence he asked to be excused and was observed to be very upset as he left the court. Clara having been shown up as a liar by her Father, became hysterical, screaming "Oh my poor Father" and dramatically collapsed in court (like they do)

Maria Castle produced Sidney's clothes in court. Several neighbours, plus the union matron and Mrs Siphert, all gave evidence, most said the corpse hair was too dark to be Sidney's but it was thought that a year in the soil had stained it dark. Clara refused to say much but still maintained she had just given Sidney away to this imaginary Mrs Henry. Unfortunately she wasn't pressed to explain herself or her lies.

Without a confession by Clara, despite the evidence and her being proven to be a liar, the Jury chose to find Clara Brockman NOT guilty on the grounds that it could not be proven that the dead child was hers - A ridiculous verdict and no attempt seems to have been made to find out what had happened to baby Sidney Brockman as he was never seen again !

Jailing a murderer costs money, ignoring a murder costs nothing. Clara Brockman and her new (un-named) child seemed to have disappeared after that. The Thanet area is packed with Brockmans all of whom fill the public records for the next 100 years including several Claras who got married.

I should imagine Clara's father didn't have anything to do with the murdering bitch afterwards, having killed his grandson and shamed him in court.

James Brockman eventually became the Miller at Grange Road Windmill and lived there until his death in 1913.

The Brockmans could possibly be related to Sarah Brockman who's murder at Ramsgate is chronicled later in this book.

Family History: Clara Brockman was born June 1855 at Northwood St Peters Thanet: Parents James Brockman & Sarah Dines. Clara had six siblings; George 1849, Josiah 1853, Walter 1858, Eliza 1859, Naomi 1860 & Annie 1863.

After Clara's mother Sarah Dines died in childbirth in 1863 Clara's father, James Brockman, married his wife's cousin Mary Dines and had 7 more children, a total of 14 kids.

Sources: Thanet Advertiser 23 Feb 1877 & 30 March 1878 & 13 July 1878 plus Ancestry.com.

13.

Dead on the Beach at Margate 1880

This case made me angry. The stupidity of the coroner just beggars belief. The victim's family received zero justice and in my opinion a murderer was allowed to walk free.

The body of Elizabeth Ashley was found dead on the beach at Margate on the morning of 15 August 1880 beneath the Fort Cliff. She had last been seen in a Margate pub around 11pm the previous evening.

At an inquest held on the 21st August, Mr Jethro William Jones, mariner, of 2 Fort Mount, identified the body as that of his daughter Elizabeth 'Betsy' Ashley, 27, a widow. She had lived in Paradise Street Margate as a housekeeper to Mr Ancell, her late sister's husband. Jethro said he had last seen his daughter leaving the Bull Inn at 9.30pm on Saturday night as he was entering the pub. She asked her father how he was getting on and he told her she shouldn't be there. Betsy was with a man that the father didn't know but assumed was a plaster by his white clothing, the man had a felt hat and carroty (ginger) whiskers. Jethro added that he couldn't say if his daughter was sober or not but knew she was never depressed and wouldn't commit suicide, she had a boy at home only 5 years old.

Betsy had no marks or injuries on her when he last saw her but when he viewed her body the next morning he saw she had two black eyes, marks on her throat and a broken leg. A married sister of Betsy's, Jane Peel of Sydney Place, said she was with her sister in the Bull and saw her father also, Betsy told her she knew three men who were in the bar and the men bought both sisters a beer. Betsy left with one of the men, his arm around her waist, the man had a red moustache and was about 23 or 25, they walked off towards the Parade. Betsy was not seeing any man in particular. She was sober only having some ale. Jane said Betsy was quite happy and had no problems at home with Mr John Ancell.

Henry Downes, ginger with a moustache, a carpenter living at the Alexander pub near St Johns Church, said he had met Betsy on the Thursday and had an ale with her at the Hall-by-the-sea. They arranged to meet at the Bull on Saturday at 8.30pm. Betsy had an ale and was sober, then they walked to the Mulberry Tree (pub) and had some pop (lemonade) and then they walked to the Ship Inn and he left her there about 10.30. He claimed they had arranged to meet on the Sunday night but she never showed up, he now knew it was because she had died.

John Ancell said he had last seen Betsy at 7.30 when she was going out, there was no relationship between them other than her being housekeeper to himself and his children. He said he went to bed at 10pm with his children. At half after midnight his daughter asked him to check the door as she had heard a noise. No one was around and he was concerned a bit that Betsy had still not come home.

Doctor White said he had examined the body and concluded the eyes were blacked before death, the nose was broken as were the cheekbones and a leg was broken also. There were bruises to the throat that were made before death. It was his opinion that the facial injuries had been caused prior to the fall but as there was water in the lungs he could only state that Elizabeth Ashley had died by drowning. The man who found her stated that when he found the body it was lying face down in very soft sand, it was wet as the tide had washed over it during the night.

Many witnesses came forward to say they had seen Betsy in the company of three men that night. The last to see her at 10.40pm was a Mrs Amy Arnold of King Street who saw Betsy with a man who looked like Henry Downes in the courtroom, Betsy was staggering a bit and the man was pulling her along up Fort Hill. She didn't seem to want to go up the Hill but he was forcing her.

Unbelievably the inquest decided there was no evidence that anyone had caused Betsy's death so they returned a verdict of accidental drowning - Quite shocking. Betsy had clearly been beaten half to death, thrown from a height down onto the beach and left unconscious to drown when the tide came in. I hope the murderer had nightmares of being caught for the rest of his miserable life.

Source: Thanet Advertiser 21 August 1880: Reynolds's Newspaper 29 August 1880 and an assortment of papers in the British newspaper archives.

Paradise Street Margate was another area that was demolished in 1939. It ran from the harbour winding up hill behind the Metropole Hotel and was the route of the tram line.

Hall-by-the-Sea was George Sanger's exotic animal circus and entertainment venue. This was later rebuilt as Dreamland.

An amazing collection of photographs were reproduced by Thanet news here;

https://theisleofthanetnews.com/2017/10/02/rare-collection-of-19th-century-hall-by-the-sea-owner-lord-sanger-to-go-under-the-hammer/

Pubs: The original Bull, the Mulberry Tree and the Ship hotel have all been demolished.

14.

Tragedy in a Northwood Cottage 1886

On an August evening in 1886, Farmer George Packer was upstairs in his Northwood house having a wash, he was looking forward to a good night out. It was about 7.45pm, a warm evening, and the window was open. Suddenly the air was filled with the sound of children screaming and the noise was getting louder and closer.

George went downstairs and opened his front door. Immediately he was beckoned outside by Mr Setterfield, his waggoner. "Here Sir, you're wanted, come here." Two children were running towards him and he instantly recognised them as Richard Revell's kids, their hysterical Mother was behind them. When she reached Mr Packer she collapsed into his arms crying that her husband had done away with himself and their babies. Packer and his waggoner ran straight to the Revell's cottage. Eliza Revell and the children followed on.

Richard Revell was a 58 year old labourer. He lived in a small cottage that stood apart on George Packer's Farm at Northwood near to the Hare and Hounds Pub. He had once worked for Packer but was now a sick man and could no longer work at all. Packer had allowed him to stay on in the cottage as he had a wife and eight children. His wife Elizabeth Revell worked very hard as a laundress and was the only breadwinner of the family of ten.

On the day in question she had left home at 11.30am to go to Mrs Bishops at St Peter's (Margate) to do the washing there. Just after 7pm two of her children, John (9) and Sarah (7) came to her saying that Father wanted her to come home straight away as he was feeling ill. Mrs Revell hurried home only to find the cottage doors locked and the blinds pulled down. Young John got in the kitchen window and called back to his Mother "Here, Father is laying on the floor" Eliza, thinking her husband had collapsed, then climbed in, only to be confronted with the horrific scene of her husband, and worst still her two babies, lying in pools of their own blood on the kitchen floor. All three had slit throats. Instinctively she snatched up the youngest, a boy of just 6 months, and cradled him in her arms praying he was not dead. But it was no use, the child was already stone cold as was the other baby. Eliza (mother) John and Sarah had then run to the farmer for help.

Once farmer George and his waggoner had reached the cottage Eliza once again picked up the youngest baby, sobbing uncontrollably as she cradled it tight. George Packer, assuming that Richard Revell was dead, attempted to find signs of life in the other infant, a little girl aged three. She too had had her windpipe severed. Sadly George realised he could be of no help to either child. Then suddenly to everyone's surprise, Richard Revell let out a groan and moved his arms. George quickly wrapped a cloth around Revell's neck but then realised the slit in the throat bled all the more by doing this, so he removed it and placed a cushion under his head to tilt it forward and close the wound. Another labourer and his wife were now at the scene and Packer ordered them to hurry and fetch Dr Raven and then to fetch Revells brother, Foster Revell, who lived nearby. Elizabeth Revell was now in deep shock, she began to rock back and forth with her dead baby in her arms, she was still holding it tight and sobbing when the doctor eventually arrived.

Three policemen duly arrived too, and having taken statements, they decided to stay all night with Richard, now their prisoner of sorts, and because it was felt the distraught family should not be left alone. The two dead children were placed in the parlour and relatives were summoned to comfort Eliza and take charge of the remaining five children (three more had since come home from being on an errand) their eldest boy, Henry (16) was living and working and away from home at the time.

Rather than stitching Revell's neck Dr Raven only bandaged it and by doing so only drew more blood loss from his patient. (George Packer could have told him that would happen) Deciding Revell's condition was far too serious for him to go to hospital, the incompetent doctor then ordered Revell to be placed on a bed and proceeded to administer his own 'cure'. Dr Raven proclaimed to the packed cottage that 'nourishment' was what was needed and lots of it! Had Dr Raven bothered to ask the children, he would have learned that Richard Revell had not long since had his tea with his children and so had already eaten. But no, Raven called for thin broth and proceeded to spoon the soup into Revell's mouth, appearing to be fascinated when it seeped out of his open neck. (Obviously anatomy was not his strong point) His next cunning plan was to insert a rubber tube up Revell's nose and attempt to manipulate it down the neck and so create a new windpipe. (fact it wouldn't be attached to the lungs didn't concern him a jot) He nigh on killed the patient on the spot. The crazy Dr Raven then declared he at last had the answer! And rolling Revell over he injected the soup up Revell's backside in his staunch belief that a bowel full of soup would set the patient right in no time. (I think he had mistaken bowl of soup for a bowel of soup somewhere in his education) The next day, the bum full of soup not bringing a miraculous cure to Revell's slit throat, Dr Raven reluctantly threw in the towel and sent his nearly dead patient to hospital. Heaven knows what those witnessing Dr Raven's medical skills must have thought of his farcical performance. Fortunately the surgeon at the hospital had a brain rather than a bum fetish and quickly stitched up Revell's throat wound.

Two days after the tragedy an inquest was opened and immediately news came to the sitting inquest that Mrs Revell was too upset to attend as her husband had just died within the hour. The Coroner was adamant in the necessity of Elizabeth Revell giving evidence and so the inquest was adjourned. Richard Revell had nodded his agreement to seeing his wife in his last moments and Elizabeth had held his hand and told him that she knew he had not meant to do what he did, she forgave him as he passed away. When the inquest was resumed a few days later, all witnesses gave testimony as to the events of the dreadful day. There was never any question of an outside person having perpetrated the crime. The Revells' eldest daughter, Mary (15) was a sensible girl and was allowed to speak in person. After her Mum had gone to work, her Father had been quiet all day. He had not been able to work for a long time as he was too ill. He was therefore often upset that their Mum had to work so hard because of him. On that day, he had complained a lot of pains in his side and was very depressed. 'Dad' had given the children their lunch and tea and insisted everyone ate in silence as he seemed lost in thought. Mary said he sat quietly after tea, playing with the youngest and bouncing the baby on his knee till around 6pm when he told her and another sister to go to Ramsgate. They often went. It was a long walk and they had to collect washing. Their Mum took in washing at home as well as going out to do washing for other people. That was the last time she had seen her little sister and baby brother alive. Richard Revell had never hurt or attempted to harm any of his children before. Dr Raven stated that Richard had been ill for a long time and he himself had been treating the man for his indigestion (no wonder he was still ill) Foster Revell identified the cut throat razor found in the kitchen covered in blood, it was Richard's own and had been given to him by their father. Foster also identified the two dead children as being that of his brother's kids. Elizabeth was too distraught to view the bodies of her babies again but named the children as Ellen Esther aged 3 years 10 months & William George aged 6 months.

It was a simple case and the verdict was no surprise. The two infants were murdered by their father Richard Revell who had since committed self destruction whilst the balance of his mind was disturbed. The only surprise came when the coroner then said the most inappropriate thing he could say. He told the court that he believed that in days of old a person committing felo de se (felon of himself) would then be buried at midnight at a crossroads with a stake through their heart to stop their ghost from rising, and although he understood the brutal practise had now been done away with, he thought that in such verdicts today the body should be quickly buried without a service. (Talk about distressing the widow even more!)

The jury were more sympathetic and personally collected 12 shillings amongst themselves to be given to Elizabeth to help feed her surviving six children. That was about 2 weeks wages for an agricultural labourer.

Family Search: Richard Revell born 1828 St Peters Nr Broadstairs Thanet son of John & Sarah Revell. Unknown whom his first wife was, but he was recorded as unmarried in the 1851 census and living with parents and widowed by the 1871 census and living with his niece Elizabeth Bartlett and two children. (both in Mother's maiden name)

In 1872 he married his niece Elizabeth Bartlett and had 6 more children. The children were: (Henry Charles 1870 & Mary 1871 both births registered as Bartlett) then Mildred 1873, Eliza 1875, John 1877, Sarah 1880, Ellen 1883, William 1886. All 8 children used Revell as their surname.

In 1872 it was not illegal for a man to marry his niece and I think that hasn't changed, but it was frowned upon by most families and the wider community.

Elizabeth Bartlett born 1847 Eastry nr Canterbury Kent daughter of John & Sarah Bartlett. Sarah seems to have been Richard Revell's sister.

Sources: The Thanet Advertiser 14 Aug 1886 Plus other news accounts at the British Newspaper Archive and Ancestry.com

15.

Richardson the Spree Shooter 1888

On New years day 1888, about 9.20pm, in Ramsgate, a man named Allen William Richardson accosted a young woman in George Street Ramsgate by the Sanger's Circus & Theatre, crying out "You're the girl!" He then fired two shots at the woman, both of which luckily missed the girl's arm. The girl was a Miss Corben. Richardson then turned to a man of the Salvation Army that was approaching and also fired at him with the gun. Again Richardson's aim was bad with the bullet narrowly missing the gentleman's head.

The loud report of the gun shots brought an immediate crowd who began to pursue Richardson down the street. As they were soon close on his heels, Richardson stopped at the corner of Thomson's passage and shouted "This is all the servant girl's fault" he began to fire at the crowd with his revolver. A lad named Charles Pillow, 21, was hit in the chest and fell down. Members of the crowd immediately picked him up, rushing him to a surgeon. Police constable Sandon and a few of the brave crowd pursued Richardson as he ran to a house in Duncan Road named the Sycamores. Richardson quickly appeared at the upstairs front window with a double barrelled shotgun. After screaming at the crowd below to "Stand back!" and they not doing as he bid, Richardson discharged the gun into the throng. Amongst the onlookers were a Mr William Fox, Mr Alfred Moody and Mr George Pillow, a brother of the lad hit earlier, all of which received gunshot injuries. The injured were conveyed to Ramsgate infirmary for immediate attention.

George Pillow had received lead shot in the shoulder and forehead but luckily the wounds were not deep enough to prove fatal, the shot was removed and he was soon allowed home. Alfred Moody received shot full in the face and was not

expected to live. William Fox sustained a shot in the head and was considered critical.

More police were summoned to the scene of the siege and soon ten constables were assembled. With shoulders to the front door they successfully smashed their way into the house, which Richardson had hastily barricaded with furniture, and bravely overpowered the deranged shooter. The public were extremely pleased to see the mad man apprehended and cheered as he was carted off to Ramsgate police cells.

It turns out that Richardson's maid had left him earlier that day to meet her fiancée. Richardson was obsessed with the young maid, possibly named Amy, and thought she was leaving his house forever and so Richardson had set off to find her (and shoot her obviously)

On Thursday 26 Jan at 5.50pm, Charles Pillow, the first guy to be shot, died from his injuries. The lad had rallied a little over the previous week but the bullet in his chest could not be excavated and remained inside. A subsequent post-mortem showed the bullet had entered his chest and lodged against his spine.

The Sycamores, Duncan Rd, Ramsgate.
Scene of the Siege

Alfred Moody, who was also uncle to Miss Corben, the first girl fired at, was sadly blinded for life and spent a long time recuperating in hospital as did William Fox who's near fatal head wound had shattered his skull. His wound hole was marvellously repaired eventually with a genuine silver plate being inserted beneath the skin, which in later years he would tap with his knuckles to prove it was there much to the fascination of viewers.

On Wednesday 1 Feb 1888 Richardson was charged at Ramsgate Police Court in the Town Hall with the murder of Charles Sydney Pillow and the attempted murder of Alfred Moody a fly coach driver, George Pillow and William Fox a pub pot man. Richardson's defence was that he was not in his right mind at the time of the shooting. He was sent to be held in Canterbury gaol until his trial at Maidstone Assizes. At Canterbury gaol it was considered that Richardson should be confined privately in an asylum as he was acting manic and it was suspected he would likely try to do himself an injury. At St Augustine's secure asylum Richardson did indeed have another fit of mania but did not injure himself, he seriously assaulted one of the warders there and injured him instead.

The evil Richardson was 37, a married man, who's wife had recently left him. He was of independent means (income from inheritance and stocks) and he even owned a yacht moored in Ramsgate harbour.

When Richardson was taken to Maidstone Court to be tried, Dr Hoar of Maidstone Prison, Dr Forbes Winslow and Dr Savage of Bethlem Asylum all stated that they had examined Richardson and agreed that he was insane and unfit to plead. The court then instructed Richardson to be incarcerated in an asylum for the criminally insane for an undetermined period.

Another sad aspect of this case is that Allen Richardson outlived all of his victims. Having murdered one and ruined the lives of three other poor souls the madman was eventually released from Broadmoor, lived to be 83 years old and died in July 1934. He was buried 23 July at Reigate in Surrey where he had been living in luxury, unlike his victims who lived the remainder of their lives in poverty and ill health relying on charity.

Family Research:

Allen William Richardson. Born December 1850 Croydon Surrey. His parents were William Ruskin Richardson 1806-1887 and Ann Maria

Mitchell 1817-1872. William Richardson was a silk trimmings manufacturer. He had been previously married to a woman named Mary McCarthy and had other children but when he died he left his fortune to just the children of his second marriage, a legacy of £89k. Those children were Allen's siblings; John J Richardson b1853, Janet Mitchell Richardson b1858 and Henry Longford Richardson b1860 all three of whom had moved to Australia. Allen Richardson was educated at a private school in Brighton. In 1871 he is recorded as an Art Student in Croydon living with his parents.

Allen Richardson's wife was Emma Kelsey 1848-1942. Marriage 23 April 1874 at Upper Norwood Croydon Surrey. The couple are recorded living in Ramsgate in 1881 at Beatrice Villas, with no children.

After his trial he was sent to Broadmoor asylum at Sandhurst in Berkshire. He is recorded there in 1891 as a patient with independent means. The actual date of his release is not known, the government never releases such details even today, but he was not recorded at Broadmoor in 1901 or in 1911 suggesting he was no longer considered insane and had been released after only a few years' confinement.

His Wife Emma Kelsey was born in Jan 1848 at Winchmore Hill Middlesex the daughter of a silk manufacturer. Parents William & Elizabeth Kelsey. She had nine siblings. Emma died 16 Nov 1942 age 94 in Caterham in Surrey and it is very likely her husband had again been living with her there.

As for his innocent victims; Alfred Moody was left blinded for life and died in Feb 1932 aged 69, for the last 20 years of his life he had been taken care of by a kindly couple named Coleman at Cliftonville Ave. Mr Moody was previously a member of the Excelsior Minstrel players, after the shooting a benefit concert was given by the minstrels in the Sanger's Hall for the wounded. Alfred gave an interview just before he died where in he believed Richardson was still in prison getting his just deserts, he had no idea he had been released years ago.

Charles Sidney Pillow: Born Oct 1865 in Canterbury. Parents Edward John Pillow & Ellen Sarah Geering. In 1881 the family had moved to Ramsgate where Charles was an errand boy and his father a decorative paper hanger. He had seven siblings plus younger brother George Pillow who was also shot. Charles died 26 Jan 1888

William Fox: It was impossible to say for sure which William fox was the gentleman who was shot as there were several men of that name living with their families in Ramsgate. He was variously described in news accounts as a muffin man, a pot man, a postman and a boatman. There was a boatman named Fox listed in the 1881 census living there with his wife Fanny & children. Whether this was the injured man or not is unknown.

Sources: Illustrated police News 7 Jan and 4 Feb 1888. Gloucestershire Chronicle 18 February 1888. Kent & Sussex Courier 27 January 1888. Various assortment of national newspapers & Ancestry.com.

D J Birkin

5 Cannonbury Road, Ramsgate

16.

The Murder of Little Milly Merriman 1891

Some murders are no mystery at all. The perpetrator is found at the scene and all too quickly dismissed as mentally ill and therefore not liable for their horrible deed. They usually get sent to a hospital only to be miraculously cured 6 months later and back out on the streets laughing at the soft courts. It appears humans are socially conditioned into accepting murders committed by lunatics as just unfortunate events, even pressured into feeling sorry for the murderer, but we should never forget that innocent victims continue to lose their lives because of these dangerous people being allowed to walk amongst us.

Little Millicent Violet Merriman was only three years old when she lost her precious life. A beautiful, engaging child with blonde curly locks and a winning smile. Milly was loved by everyone that met her and she had every right to grow up and lead a long and happy life. Her own Mother tore that right from her in the most evil way she could, deliberately slicing the innocent child's throat for no reason at all.

Newman Merriman and his wife Mary lived at 5 Cannonbury Road Ramsgate. The Merrimans seemed happily married and never appeared to argue and had no money troubles as Newman had investments and was already financially independent by his mid 20s. Mary's parents, Edwin and Anna Martin, were retired and had come to live with the couple and so with little 'Milly' the loving family of five rubbed along very comfortably.

Around Christmas time 1890 Mary began complaining of headaches, she said she was sure she was going mad. The doctor saw her several times and prescribed rest and sal volatile - a solution of ammonium carbonate in ammonia water and alcohol, but the headaches continued and Mary's demeanour began to change. She would often state she was dying, saying she was frightened but didn't know what of. She begged her husband not to leave her alone in case 'something happened'. Other times she would be too frightened to go to sleep and wandered about the house in the middle of the night not knowing what she was doing. Sadly the family thought it was not serious enough to consult a 'doctor of the mind.' Perhaps they feared she would be committed to an asylum against their wishes.

The Mother, Mrs Martin, had taken over all of the household chores when her daughter had first started to feel unwell. To help Mary cope, Newman had taken on a nursemaid at Christmas to look after little Milly so his wife could rest. Today a doctor would probably request a brain scan to see if a tumour might be present, but this was 1890 and headaches were seen as a symptom of worry, over indulgence or even just as women's hysterics. Aspirin had not been invented as such at this time and the usual painkiller prescribed was still Laudanum, the highly addictive tincture of Opium. Strangely there was never any mention of Mary Merriman being prescribed this drug which suggests that her headaches were not that regular or severe. Her sanity though was becoming an increasing worry to her family.

The nursemaid, Caroline Bailey, having only been with the family a short time, noticed a marked decline in Mary's behaviour, her mistress seemed constantly restless often asking her not to go out or even to leave the room. It seems in hindsight that Mary didn't trust herself to be left alone. Schizophrenics often hear voices inside themselves urging them to do things against their will and so fear being left alone with these voices in case they can't resist them. Whether Mary's illness was mental or physical we will never know but in August 1891 she could fight her urges no longer.

On the 2nd of August 1891 Mrs Martin was cooking the Sunday lunch. Her husband Edwin and son in law Newman decided to go for a long walk and work up an appetite. They encouraged Mary to go with them saying the fresh air would do her good, Caroline the nursemaid could bring Milly and they would all stroll along the beach towards Pegwell Bay. Mary agreed and the family set off. Turning left into Grange Road, by the old windmill, it was but a short walk to the beach but the party had only walked as far as a public bench in Grange Rd when Mary announced her desire to sit down and rest. They had walked less than a hundred yards. After a moment's rest Mary then announced that she couldn't go any further and was going to return home. (This would suggest she had already formulated her plan at this point.) Her Father and husband offered to escort her back home but Mary insisted they carry on with their walk and only Caroline the maid and little Milly should return with her. (again premeditation) As Mary and Caroline turned back into Cannonbury road, Mary began walking faster leaving the maid and child behind. She seemed to be in a hurry. Caroline was carrying Milly as she seemed sleepy. Reaching the house first, Mary went round the back alley, through the kitchen at the rear of the house and opened the front door for Caroline. (why didn't she knock as her Mother was there) She then told Caroline to quickly take the baby straight up to the nursery bedroom on the top floor. Mary followed them. Once there, Caroline stood Milly down and was instructed by Mary to go straight back downstairs to the kitchen and get hot water and the sal volatile as she had a headache. (again premeditated action) Caroline did as she was told and after a few minutes returned with the boiled water and medicine. The door to the bedroom was now shut and so Caroline knocked. She could hear footsteps inside and tried the door knob but the door was locked. Caroline called out to Mary to let her in, but was ignored. Suspecting something was wrong with her mistress she went round through the adjacent bedroom and entered by the second door which Mary had forgotten to lock. As Caroline entered, Mary ran across the room to one of the front windows, which she had already opened wide, and started to climb out. Caroline grabbed hold of Mary's skirt as Mary dangled in mid air over the window sill. Caroline screamed "what are you doing, where's Milly?" to which Mary replied "I've killed her." As Caroline looked over her shoulder she now saw Milly slumped like a rag doll against a box on the floor, her neck bleeding. The horrified little nursemaid could no longer hold onto her mistress' skirt and Mary fell to the ground outside, a fall of less than twelve feet, but head first.

The distraught young maid rushed to Milly's aid but could see it was already too late, the little girl's head was nearly severed. Flying downstairs, to find Mrs Martin in the kitchen, (who must have been bloody deaf) the two women then ran outside to help Mary who was now lying on the path by the front door. Two neighbours opposite had seen Mary fall from the window and had hastened to assist. Soon a small crowd had gathered at the scene, several men ran off to fetch a doctor. Mary was conscious but had a broken leg and bleeding head. There was a yellow staining around her mouth suggesting she had also taken some unknown substance.

It was nearly 12 noon and Mr Merriman and his Father-in-law decided to give up on their walk and return home for lunch. As they turned into Cannonbury road they saw a crowd outside their house and were beckoned to hurry. Running to Mary's side Newman asked Mary if she recognised him, Mary said she did and told him "I am dying. You have been a kind husband to me and will be happier when I am gone." The doctor had sort assistance when first summoned, but as no other doctor was available he procured several police constables to assist him. The doctor had Mary carried inside the house and due to the staining on her lips he suspected she had swallowed iodine, which is not usually a fatal substance but he still got the police to help him pump out Mary's stomach. The doctor had rushed up to see Milly the instant he had arrived and realised there was nothing to be done for the child. Mary's broken leg was then splinted and she was soon on her way to hospital.

The surgeon who examined Mary at the hospital diagnosed a fracture in the skull but was more concerned with the large dilation of Mary's eyes and the absence of any pain. He suspected she had taken a large dose of Belladonna and quickly had her stomach completely washed out again. This poison is a plant better known in the countryside as Deadly Nightshade. Every part of the plant is highly toxic. A liquid extract used in small quantities was in olden times used as an anaesthetic. In Victorian times it was still commonly applied with a dropper to the eyes of ladies to make the pupils enlarge which in turn makes them appear more alluring. This cosmetic application gave the plant its Latin name Belladonna meaning 'beautiful lady'. It was commonly available without prescription at any chemist for use in the eyes only. Large doses of ingested Belladonna are fatal but due to its anaesthetic property it is not a poison that causes extremes of agony. Mary seemed very calm. When asked if she knew what she had done to her daughter, she said "yes I killed her" but then didn't want to say anything else and began to lose consciousness. The poison had already taken hold of Mary, lingering a few hours more; she then died peacefully.

So Mary Merriman was dead because she wanted to be so. Milly had not had a choice. Mary had wilfully planned and executed the murder of her beautiful child for no justifiable reason. She could just as easily have chosen to kill only herself and left Milly with her family that day. Mary professed to love her husband yet had deliberately destroyed his life too in the most evil way she could by slaughtering his only and beloved child. And it was cold blooded slaughter. Mary had with forethought planned the crime so she could be in the house without her husband and father to prevent her carrying out her plan. Mary had also, with premeditated intent, concealed a sharp kitchen knife upstairs in the bedroom before going out that day with the express intention of using it on Milly and had even rushed home as if she was excited by the thought of killing her child and could barely wait to do it. Mary had made sure she had a painless sleepy death whilst inflicting a painful horrific and terrifying death on poor Milly.

It's impossible to know the twisted thoughts that ran through that evil woman's mind. Mary could have heard voices telling her Milly was the devil or some benign creature that needed destroying or more likely as it was a premeditated act she had planned to crush her husband, we'll never know what her spiteful reason was. Tragically her husband, Newman Merriman, was left in a living hell. He was a heartbroken and emotionally shattered man. The poor man buried his wife and child in Ramsgate then moved to London kindly taking his elderly in-laws with him. When old Mr Martin (Mary's dad) died Newman looked after his mother in law until she too passed away. He never married again and spent the rest of his days alone in different lodging houses until he died in 1920, he was only 58 years old.

The autopsies showed Milly had had her throat cut twice with extreme force, the first cut was sufficient to have killed the child. Mary had Belladonna in her stomach but iodine only in her mouth, she may have baulked at the taste and spat it out. She had a fracture in her skull and a broken leg and bruising from her fall, but her death came from the Belladonna poison. The surgeon conducting the post mortem said he noticed 'some softening of the brain' which in his opinion eventually can lead to insanity in some cases but he didn't think it had progressed that far, no tumours were noted.

The verdict of the inquest was that Mary had wilfully murdered Millicent and committed suicide whilst insane.

Family research:

Newman Frederick Merriman born July 1862 Dorchester Dorset and died on 6 Nov 1920 of cancer in St John's nursing home Camden Sq. Middlesex. Newman left an estate of £167 to his sister Julia Frances Merriman. His father was Edward Merriman 1821-1869 a Carpenter and his mother Emily Mayo 1826-1875. He had six siblings: Lewis 1860-1943, Herbert 1866, Emma 1855, Henrietta 1857, Emily 1861 & Julia 1868.

Mary fannie Nielsine Merriman was born in Denmark in 1865. She and Newman had married 30 Dec 1884 in London.

Her Father was a draper and did business in Denmark and that is where he had met his Danish wife. They were Edwin Martin born 1830 in Bath and Anna (maiden name unknown possibly Nielsine) born in Denmark in 1840 according to census records.

Millicent Violet Merriman was born 10 July 1888 in Ramsgate. She died 2nd Aug 1891 and was buried on 6th Aug in Ramsgate Cemetery in the same grave as her Mother. Milly had a white cloth covered coffin with silver furniture.

Sources: Thanet Advertiser 8 Aug 1891, The Courier 7 Aug 1891 plus assortment of newspapers at The British news archive. Family research at the IGI and Ancestry.com.

17.

Who Killed Mrs Noel 1893

This is a famous unsolved case and best summed up by paraphrasing Sir Arthur Conan Doyle from his story, Silver blaze.

When Inspector Gregory asks "Is there any other point to which you would wish to draw my attention?"

Sherlock Holmes replies "To the curious incident of the dog in the night-time".

"The dog did nothing in the night-time." exclaims Gregory.

"That was the curious incident." replies Holmes.

I am an extremely cynical person, much to the annoyance of my family. Within minutes of seeing a husband or relative on TV making a sobbing (but dry eyed) plea for the murderer of their beloved to come forward, I nearly always declared they did it themselves. More often than not it turns out that they were the killer or in cahoots with the killer. It's not difficult to spot a faker clutching a handful of bone dry tissues, they always over act and there's never a trace of tears on their faces, especially the wives and mothers with un-smudged perfect make-up and a fresh hair-do pleading for their supposedly *kidnapped* children. If my child or spouse had ever been abducted or killed I can guarantee I would have to be physically held up by two doctors. I'd be covered in snot and tears and would look like the Wreck of the Hesperus – Certainly not swanning around Portugal playing tennis with my pals. I can smell liars a mile off.

I make no apology for my belief, and that of the police at the time of this particular case, that the husband was the murderer. Had I chosen to become a copper I dare say I would have gained a reputation for being a hard bastard. The police are employed to fight for the victims that have no voice not mamby pamby the lying criminals. I would have hounded William Noel, the husband in this account, to his grave and pushed to have investigated the deaths of all 4 of his infant children too, demanding to see their death certificates and supposed graves.

William and Sarah Dinah Noel lived at 9 Adelphi Terrace, Grange Road Ramsgate (now numbered 20 Grange Rd) At the front of the building was a shop where William Noel carried on his business as a butcher. The couple lived on the premises, behind and above the shop. The couple had been married 15 years and Mrs Noel was 10 years older than her husband. He was 43, she 53. Before coming to Ramsgate the Noels had lived in Portsmouth where Mrs Noel had owned a lodging house with her sister Elizabeth, then both women were of the maiden name Saunders. Noel had been a butcher's delivery man and had wooed Sarah whilst delivering her meat orders, eventually marrying her and borrowing money from her father to buy into the guest house business. They had two children, separate events, both of whom had died shortly after birth before their births could be registered, and interestingly the deaths went unregistered too. (Testimony of the births was later provided by the sister Elizabeth.)

After persuading his new wife to sell the lodging house, the Noel's moved to Ramsgate and used what money they made of their share in the business to purchase the butchers shop. They had been paid in Portsmouth to foster a little orphaned boy, naturally the boy was dumped back on the workhouse when then moved to Ramsgate as selling the lodging house meant William Noel didn't need the boys rent money now he had his own business.

The Noels now lived alone and employed a servant girl named Nelly Wilson, aged 16, to come in every day to do the housework. Three males also worked for Noel in his business. These were two older chaps who helped with the lamb slaughtering and cutting up the meat in the rear outhouse and a young delivery boy. The Noels also owned a large black retriever dog called Nip.

The morning of 14 May 1893 was the same as most Sundays in the Noel household. William and Sarah attended chapel service in the morning then returned home for dinner. The maid Nelly would spend the morning cleaning and preparing vegetables and then stay and have dinner with the Noels. She would then have the afternoon off to go to Sunday school for a while. (This was common, most teens went to Sunday school. It was a way to meet friends like a social club.) Nelly didn't live with the Noels, she lived nearby with her parents at 5 King Herman Terrace. The three male employees didn't usually work on Sundays and neither did they ever enter the house, only the shop.

Six years previous both Sarah and William had attended the Hardress Street Chapel together, but there had been some unpleasantness with Noel being accused of inappropriate behaviour, kissing and groping young girls. Since then Sarah had continued to go to the Hardress chapel alone (no loyalty to her husband then) and William had changed his attendance to the St Lawrence Wesleyan Chapel. William was a server there and treasurer at his new chapel and took the plate round for collection. His wife Sarah kept the books for their butchery business and also did the treasury accounts for the money collected at William's chapel and her own chapel. Sarah held all the purse strings in the couple's life.

On Sunday 14 May 1893, after dinner, Nelly cleared up the dinner things and Mr Noel went into the downstairs sitting room/office to gather his books. He was going to chapel to give an afternoon Sunday school lesson which he did every Sunday. Mrs Noel asked her husband for that morning's chapel collection money and he gave her about 10 shillings (today that's 50p) There were no bad words spoken between the couple in Nelly's presence and then Nelly left the house as was usual at 2pm by the back scullery door, she passed Mrs Noel as she went. (the kitchen in those days was like a dining room with table and chairs and a large black iron cooking stove, washing up was done next door in a tiny scullery with a stone sink and cold water tap)

Sometime after Nelly left, Sarah Noel was shot dead in the kitchen of her own house. The murderer was never brought to justice. William Noel claimed that his wife was alive when he left home for the Sunday School. He claimed that after dinner he had gone to the sitting room/office and had given Sarah the chapel collection money and then Nelly had left. Sarah had then gone upstairs to the private sitting room above the shop (now a front bedroom) and he never saw her, or spoke to her again before leaving the house. (not even a goodbye)

Noel claimed he had left the house at 2pm, literally after Nelly. He said he had left by the door into the alley (known as the front door) the key had been in the lock in the inside of the door, he had had no need to remove the key or lock the door as his wife was at home.

Mrs Lavinia Squires who lived opposite the Noels later stated that she saw William Noel from her upstairs sitting room window outside his house at 2.20pm not 2pm and he walked off in the direction of going to chapel. (20 minute discrepancy)

The Wesleyan Chapel was a short 5 minute walk away in Chapel Road on the corner of Forge Lane (it's still there)

Arthur Rowe, secretary of the Sunday school, stated that Noel arrived at 2.25pm not 2.05pm as Noel claimed. (again 20 minute discrepancy) Nelly, who had gone to meet friends, also saw Mr Noel at the Sunday school when he arrived just before 2.30pm (3rd person to confirm the 20 minute discrepancy in Noel's story) and he was outside the chapel talking with three young girls (teenagers) when Nelly left chapel at 3.40pm. She then spent some time chatting with her friends. Later, Nelly, heading home with her girlfriends, was stopped in Grange Road by Noel who was now with another young woman, he said " I can't get indoors Nelly, if you see Mrs Noel will you tell her." Nelly said she would and went home.

Noel's Butchery Shop Today. The Side Door in the Alley has been blocked up. The stable & slaughter house remain.

In those days 9 Adelphi terrace had a side front door to the private accommodation in the side alley (today it's blocked up) this removed any necessity to open the shop and go through it out of business hours. After leaving Sunday school Noel claimed he went straight home and found this side front door locked, this was unusual as it was only locked at night and Mrs Noel was supposedly indoors. There was only one door key and Noel claimed he didn't have it and it should have been in the door on the inside. Noel said he knocked several times and rang the bell twice which set the dog off barking loudly. He then tried the scullery door round the back which was also mysteriously locked and that made the dog bark even more. He claimed he then put his church books in his horse stable in the backyard and went out to the front street to see if his wife was about, which is when he had seen and spoken to Nelly and some other girls.

Now for the weird bit: Not finding his wife, Noel fetched a step ladder from the stable and put it up to the back kitchen window, the dog was barking madly not being able to see who was outside because of the lace curtain. The dog barked ferociously at any person coming to the house. Noel apparently 'knew' the kitchen sash window was not locked and so he slid down the top half of the sash and looked in, telling the dog to be quiet. He saw his wife lying on the floor in front of the far kitchen door and the dog was sitting next to her.

So if the window was unlocked why did Noel even use a ladder? The window is on the ground floor. Why didn't he just slide up the bottom half of the sash and quickly rush in to attend to his wife on the floor who might only have been sick? Why open only the top half when both halves slide up and down when the lock is off? In my lifetime I must have lived in over half a dozen terraced houses just like the Noel's house. The back ground floor sash window is always set low, you can just sit on the sill and swing your legs over into the back yard with no need to jump, climb or use a ladder. Bizarrely, Noel next decided to climb down the ladder and rather than get into his house to help his wife he went off to find a neighbour (a witness) It was now about 4.20pm.

Noel '*finding*' his wife dead

Mr James Harman lived next door at number 8, he was in the dairy trade and had lived there 3 and a half years. Despite their front doors being opposite each other in the alley Noel had not spoken to Harman for two years, both had contracted a bad debt and Noel had not spoken to him since. Now Noel was at Harman's door saying "I think my wife is dead or something, come and have a look".

Harman, very surprised by this request, especially as Noel didn't appear distressed in any way, climbed the ladder as instructed by Noel and looked in at Mrs Noel. She was near the open kitchen door that led to the sitting room/office behind the shop. The dog barked at Harman. Noel, now he had his witness in place, pulled up the bottom sash and climbed in the window, telling the dog to shut up; he then unbolted the scullery door and let Mr Harman in. So why didn't he pull up the bottom sash to start with? Because he didn't want to go in without his witness.

Harman said Mrs Noel was obviously dead and had been shot in the side of the head. There was a pool of blood on the floor but no sign of a gun. Harman said he'd fetch a doctor. Noel said "get Dr Fox he's my doctor" Harman left on his errand leaving by the scullery door because the front door was locked and the key missing from it – Noel now alone easily had a few minutes to hide the key upstairs. (I believe he had it in his pocket all along.)

The Noel's dog, Nip, was a large beast, a heavy set black retriever with a docked tail. It was kept as a guard dog and barked and growled at everyone coming to the premises as was its job. Like most guard dogs they can be friendly when away from home and not needing to protect their master or their home. Dogs are very intelligent. During the week Noel kept it in the back sitting room/office of the shop. Nelly had been told never to go near it on her own again for she had once done so and it had bitten her arm. It was also known to have bitten two other people that came into the house. When it barked at staff or customers Noel would shout at it and it would slink off and lie down at his command. When anyone visited the house, the dog would be put in another room but when taken for a walk it would be friendly as it wasn't then guarding the house.

So now we have a very strange crime scene: Mrs Noel dead by the kitchen door which led to the sitting room/office and also to the front door which was locked with no key, and the shop was all locked up, so the murderer could not have left that way. The back door in the scullery was bolted from the inside (until Noel had opened it to let Harman in) No gun in the room and a guard dog in the same room as the corpse. The only way the murderer could have left the house was by opening the bottom half of the sash window, climbing out and then sliding it down closed afterwards, thus it still being unlocked when Noel arrived. (Why would an intruder/murderer leave by a window, and kindly close it after him, when he could have just left by the back or front door? And if he had left by the front door then who locked it after him and where was the key? Murderers don't usually lock up strangers' houses before they run off. And why was the back door bolted This seems an extremely bizarre way for an intruder to flee a scene but maybe ideal for Noel if he was his wife's killer, because if he had killed his wife and left by the scullery door then it would still have been unlocked when he returned from Sunday school and therefore he couldn't claim to be locked out...if not locked out he then wouldn't have had any reason to call a neighbour to act as a witness to him finding his wife's body by them only looking in a window without actually being in touching distance of her and therefore he could not be suspected of having been inside and killed her after his return from Sunday school.

Then there were still the curious actions of the dog. How could a stranger enter the house by the front door, lock it and remove the key, then kill Mrs Noel for some unknown reason and then bolt the scullery door from the inside for some bizarre reason and choose to leave via the window with the barking vicious dog all the time being in the same room with it's mistress? Plus no one had heard the dog barking until Noel had come home from Chapel.

Obviously the dog knew the murderer. But then it had bitten members of staff proving it was only loyal to Noel and his wife on the premises. It even barked like crazy when Noel himself was at the window behind the lace curtain because it couldn't see him. A very strange mystery indeed and worthy of our dear Sherlock.

At 4.45 Dr Fox had arrived followed shortly after by Dr Cotton. Noel was upstairs at the time and had just 'discovered' the front door key on his wife's bed (raising my eyebrows) Coming downstairs, Noel, ignoring his dead wife on the floor, pointed to an empty cash box on the kitchen floor and declared to Dr Fox "See, look, they've been there." Dr Fox sent Harman for the police. When they arrived Noel's behaviour was noted as peculiar, he was upstairs again going through his wife's processions and declaring it must have been a burglar because his wife's savings book and purse was missing with £7 in it. Inspector Ross pointed out to him that a thief would have no use for a savings book and Noel had already informed him that all Mrs Noel's jewellery was still in her room, plus Mrs Noel was still wearing, a gold watch, gold necklace chain, a brooch and 5 gold rings and in his experience thieves don't break into houses to kill a person only to take a purse and a useless savings book and leave all the gold and other obvious money in the house behind- nether do they lock up houses after themselves.

A crowd had now gathered in the alley and street outside and Noel made a point of ignoring the Inspector and going outside to inform them all loudly that his wife had been murdered by a burglar!

Mrs Noel's body was removed and the police, by now a dozen or so of them, began a four hour thorough search of the premises. They lifted every floor board in search of the gun and searched the out buildings too. They didn't find the gun. Inspector Ross was convinced by the impossible scene of locked doors, vicious dog, Noel's reactions to questions and his bizarre behaviour, that Noel had murdered his wife, but without the proverbial smoking gun he had no real evidence with which to arrest Noel. (If I was Noel I'd have planned to stuff the gun down inside one of the meat carcasses in the shop to dispose of it later, I bet the police didn't put their hands inside the meat) Noel now sent his wife's relatives the news of Sarah's death (by telegram?)

The wife's eldest sister Elizabeth and her niece Alice Simms arrived the next day. They slept in Mrs Noel's bedroom and Noel slept in his own room at the back of the house, he didn't sleep with his wife anyway. Then the next day, the 16th, an inquest was started but the police needed more time to collect evidence so the inquest was adjourned, the neighbours and some witnesses were able to give their testimonies though to save time.

Nelly and Mr Harman gave their accounts of the day as I have already related, plus several persons swore to hearing a gunshot around 2.15 and of seeing Noel at 2.20 or 2.25 leaving for chapel.

Alice King, who was the maid next door at the Harman's house, said she heard a gunshot at 2.15 but then thought maybe it was Mr Noel slamming his front door extra hard as he usually left for chapel at 2.15 or 2.20 every Sunday, not 2 o'clock.

Mr Harman said he hadn't heard a gunshot as he had been out delivering some milk and didn't come home until about 4.15 just before Noel had called on him.

Dr Fox and Dr Cotton closely observed what time rigour mortis set in on the body at the mortuary which confirmed both of their opinions that death had taken place between 2pm and 2.15pm. (So that was after Nelly left at 2pm and before Noel arrived at the chapel at 2.25pm, which was 5 mins from his house)

Before the inquest could be resumed again the police worked flat out around the clock tirelessly collecting statements, over 100 of them in writing. Despite Noel claiming that his marriage had been a happy one and him having no reason to wish for the death of his wife, a very different picture of Noel began to emerge.

People came forward to state they had often seen Noel in the company of different young women about town at night. Several farmers stated Noel often brought young women with him in his cart of an evening to buy lambs from them and one said Noel would take women walking out on the sheep marshes for hours, even picking wild flowers for them. One PC remembered seeing Noel out at night with a Miss Miller, and later Noel was still hanging about outside the woman's home in the dark when his wife came and found him and argued with him in the street about it.

William Hogben, who worked for Noel, said Noel would call on a Miss Colleen at her house and take her out riding with him blatant as anything.

A Miss Agnes Pidduck who helped at the chapel said Noel had asked her, 10 months previously, to nurse a young woman in her confinement (childbirth) for him and he would pay her; she had refused him but couldn't say what relationship Noel might have had with the lady.

A neighbour of the Noel's claimed to have walked into their butcher's shop only to see Noel and Miss Miller in a compromising position on a table in the back office, she claimed to have left disgusted and never used the butchers shop again.

It got worse when there were claims of girls being harassed and groped by Noel at his previous chapel and one lady said he grabbed her round the waist in Clarence park and tried to kiss her causing her to run all the way home to tell her mother.

Of course none of this was evidence that Noel had killed his wife, only that he was a sexual predator. If he was having an affair then that could be a motive for getting rid of his wife but there was no evidence of any particular current mistress that could be established, well not in Ramsgate anyway.

With no witness to the actual shooting and no weapon, the police had only one argument, Noel must have done it because he was the only person there at the time, even though Noel still held fast in his claim to have left home at 2pm and not 2.20 or 2.25 as witnesses had sworn.

Now another very strange thing happened. Alice Simms, the wife's niece, suddenly claimed to have found Mrs Noel's purse hidden in the bedroom drawer in the room where she was sleeping. When she gave it to Noel he declared "See the police hid it, they are testing me! He then sent for Inspector Ross and accused him of hiding the purse, or of not doing a proper search. This was totally bizarre and Inspector Ross was quite naturally perplexed...and annoyed to say the least, after all it had been Noel himself who had claimed his wife's purse was missing and the police had removed and searched all the drawers when searching for the gun even unfolding all the clothes and linens, so what was Noel playing at? Why would the police take the purse and then hide it? They were convinced from the start it was a fake robbery set up by Noel, they would have been pleased to find the purse to prove there had been no robbery, none of this made any sense. Then suddenly Noel threw up his arms dramatically and declared "I have it, I know who murdered my beloved soul" Inspector Ross then replied, I imagine sarcastically, "Go on, do tell me, who did it?" " My sister in law is the killer," announced Noel. The Inspector then asked the obvious as to why the sister, Elizabeth, would do it and Noel said because she had grievances against him and hated him. Again the Inspector asked the obvious as to why Elizabeth would kill her own sister who she rarely saw and they only wrote occasionally but in loving terms, if it was Noel that she hated, surely she would want to shoot him not her own sister. "Because she lives with a man she's not married to and is trying to pin this on me" replied Noel. "She must have stolen the purse when she killed Sarah and replaced it when she came to stay afterwards. She must have sneaked in the back door with her man and shot her" None of this made any sense at all and the police were totally confused (As I still am) Was Noel suggesting his sister in law sneaked in the back door of her own sisters house, shot her for no reason other than disliking her husband for something that happened nearly 20 years before, stole a purse, then locked the back door and climbed out the window...then brought the purse and its 5 sovereign contents back again? It seemed Noel was either insane or trying to throw blame away from himself in a bizarre way and was trying to muddy the waters by claiming the police were either crooked or incompetent. Fact was the police were not silly, they had already checked out the sister and established that she was in fact married, and had been twice since Noel knew her in Portsmouth. After her first husband died in 1886 she had married again and her name was now Mrs Harris and she was living happily with her second husband in Bexhill Sussex, she was a nurse and although she did fall out with Noel some 18 years previously over a money dispute with the lodging house they once owned jointly she wasn't still concerned about it. Mrs Harris admitted to disliking Noel but had stayed in touch with her sister and Mrs Noel had sent her and their other sisters, £5 each for every birthday (Noel didn't know any of this, his wife had never told him) also Mrs Harris had several alibis for the day Sarah was murdered, one of them her vicar, it being a Sunday. Also when she came to stay for the night after her sister died, in company with her niece, she hadn't told Noel anything of herself because she considered it none of his business. Noel had made his own erroneous assumptions about her. In the eyes of the police Noel was again confirmed as a fool and a liar.

When part two of the inquest finally ended the jury could only conclude that Mrs Noel had been murdered by a person as yet unknown. As Noel left the court the police decided to arrest him. I won't bore you with the long winded script of the trial, as I have a lot more to tell on this case, suffice to say no fresh evidence could be discovered, except more dirt on Noel being a sexual predator with lots of girlfriends, an obvious dislike for his wife and being disgruntled that she held all the purse strings not allowing him free spending of their money. Simply put, there were no witnesses to the shooting and no weapon. A gun that fitted the bullet had been found in the sea under Ramsgate cliffs by a member of the public after the inquest, but with no ballistic forensics in those days it could never be proved to be Noel's or the murder weapon. The case for the police was simply the fact that no one else but Noel could have committed the murder. Only Noel could have timed and planned it all so perfectly, his account of where he was when his wife was killed between 2pm and 2.20pm was doubted and the dog would only have let him do it and no one else. (If only dogs could speak)

Noel asked for his dog to be brought into court and said "look see how friendly he is." Because Guard dogs *away from their place of guarding*, are always fine with people, any kennels will tell you that.

Maybe the police did not have strong enough evidence to bring Noel to court at that point, I can see that, but the Judge Mr Justice Graham was still a complete arsehole. He called Inspector Ross an "Ill bread bloodhound" for not finding the purse in the drawer! (maybe that was Noel's intention in hiding the purse to make the cops look stupid in court) The judge then accused the police of being drunkards after Noel had said that during the search of his house the police had taken his bottles of beer without his permission and sat around drinking them.

Inspector Ross was furious, he swore that Noel had given his men some beer after the search because they were tired and thirsty having had no refreshment and worked non stop until 9pm at night in the house and long after their shifts should have ended. Ross then openly vowed to repay Noel the money for the beer he had given his men. The judge then rebuked Inspector Ross for not searching properly for the gun because his men were busy drinking (outrageous!!) He then asked why had the police not bothered to look in the sea for the gun so that it was left to the public to find it? Even if it wasn't the murder weapon the police should still have found it in the sea themselves apparently! Then the judge blatantly LIED (I'll explain that in a moment) and said he had received all the depositions the day before the trial and had read them carefully, twice over, and found there was no evidence in any of them, instead they were loaded with public statements that were all irrelevant (including presumably all the witnesses statements to hearing the gunshot and the witnesses that stated the whereabouts of Noel at the time of the murder?) But all that was completely irrelevant according to Justice Graham who concluded with a damming rant at the police saying "It can only be hoped that the true murderer will be detected if the police follow material clues in the future with some of the enthusiasm they have displayed in investigating irrelevant issues.

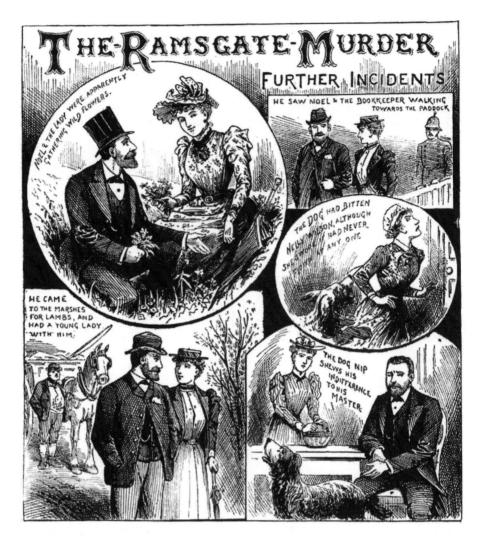

He instructed the jury to find Noel not guilty, even though the jury had already agreed amongst themselves that Noel was in fact guilty. The baffled jury had no option but to do as the Judge instructed and reluctantly declared a verdict of not guilty.

The crowded court was amazed, and angry, every one was appalled at the Judge's handling of the case and his offhanded dismissal of all the witnesses who swore Noel was at home at 2.20 and therefore home when his wife died. Noel who must have floated out of the court on cloud nine and run off to buy a lottery ticket whilst his luck was still holding.

After the trial the whole of Ramsgate and the police were in uproar. No one blamed the police and everyone was adamant that Noel had got away with murder because of the buffoon of a judge. The town magistrates, solicitors, mayor, aldermen and the county chief of police decided to get together to discuss the matter. The case had been lost but they could still criticise the judge and publicly rebuke him for his incompetence in trying the case and for his disparaging remarks made of the police and thereby express their opinion that Noel had been rightfully arrested (they had no intention of looking for anyone else) They decided the best plan was to arrange a huge testimonial dinner in honour of Inspector Ross, and his men, and invite the public to make donations. For the event they arranged for the press to be present to record all the speeches made by the town's most prominent people and record their public condemnations of Justice Graham. (I love it) Money poured in from the public along with hundreds of written testimonials in support of Ramsgate police force.

On the night of the big dinner several important local magistrates who had been involved it the case stood up and related how they had spend 16 hours just reading the depositions themselves over several days and if Justice Graham had indeed read them all, TWICE as he so claimed, then the judge managed 32 hours of non stop reading in the 24 hours the statements were in his possession neither sleeping nor taking food...or else he was a LIAR and hadn't read them which is why he dismissed them all as irrelevant. Several solicitors who had crossed swords with Justice Graham gave scathing accounts of the judge's previous examples of poor judgement, once having given a mother a sentence of 20 years penal servitude for shielding her boy who had committed a minor crime - the home secretary had to step in and reduce the sentence down to 6 months. Another time Justice Graham had dismissed the cases of 3 well known criminals and on the same day sentenced a young child to 18 months in jail for stealing a penny from a school friend. The speeches went on for ages condemning Justice Graham and praising the police, all rapturously applauded by over a hundred dinner guests and all busily recorded by the invited press. Inspector Ross was in tears as the chief of police applauded him and presented him with a £50 gold watch and silver topped cane for outstanding commitment and hard work for trying his best to bring Noel to justice.

(Let's hope copies of all the attending newspapers were posted to the judge as a sharp public rebuke.)

So what became of William Noel?

Well I had to do a lot of searching to track down our Billy the butcher. For a start he disappeared from Ramsgate immediately after his trial and changed his name which made him very hard to trace. He moved to Wimbledon Surrey (now South London) and began calling himself William Williams. He then set himself up again as a butcher with a shop at 333 Haydon Road Wimbledon. (Now he had his hands on all the finances!)

Two years later in 1895 he married Winifred Gibbs at Fulham. She was 35 and Noel was 45. Her parents had been butchers. After her father's death her Mother opened a fancy goods shop in Battersea London and both she and daughter Winifred were working there in 1891. So if Noel had met Winifred working in a gift shop after 1893 when his wife died then I feel it's a strange coincidence that her family were also once butchers, but if he had met her a few years previous whilst they were still in the butchery trade, perhaps at Smithfield meat market or when buying lambs from a farmer, then it suggests to me that maybe Noel had known Winifred before his wife's death and perhaps Winnie was the reason he wanted rid of her, but that can never be proven now.

333 Haydons Rd Wimbledon. Where William Noel moved to with his new wife and set up as William's Butchers (2nd shop in from corner)

William married Winifred Gibbs in the name of Noel so Winifred knew who he really was but they lived as Mr and Mrs Williams and the shop traded as William Williams butchers. They also filled in the 1901 census as Mr and Mrs Williams so again Winnie knew they were living a lie and hiding their identity. Not until the 1911 census did they declare, on paper, that they were Mr and Mrs Noel trading as William Williams and wife. I imagine the neighbours still called them Mr & Mrs Williams as you can see in the enclosed photo I managed to track down that William Williams is printed on the shop awning.

The 1911 census asked more questions than those previously taken. Couples now had to state length of time married and how many live births had taken place during the marriage. The Noel's stated 2 live births had taken place in their marriage and neither child was living. It turns out neither were registered either. Once again Noel had produced 2 children who had died shortly after birth as had happened with Sarah. Now you might dismiss this as the usually ill informed garbage that "Most babies used to die in infancy" but actually that is not the case born out by statistics of the period proven also by the explosion of the Victorian population. Certainly a lot of lower class families did lose a child or two before school age due to poverty, alcoholism, neglect, starvation and childhood illnesses but they also had another 8 or 12 that survived. The Noels were not barefoot ragged families living in scum alleys; they were well nourished healthy adults living in excellent accommodation who could afford the best food and doctors, so it's especially unusual to lose 4 babies and produce no other living children at all. I genuinely suspect Noel did not want children, he neither wanted the responsibility nor the financial commitment of raising children that would not benefit him in any way. Plus if he decided to bump off his wife and start afresh he wouldn't want brats cramping his style with the young ladies. I'm also deeply suspicious of four children's deaths going unregistered of both birth and death, even a dying baby was baptised by a vicar in the home. Concealment of birth from registration was a criminal offence since compulsory registration had been made law in 1837. Stillborns could go unregistered at birth but must be medically examined by a doctor, or qualified midwife. Noel's children were not stillborns as the census stated 'born alive' If a child had breathed unaided then it was deemed, in law, to have lived an independent life and the death at least must be recorded by a doctor. None of the deaths of Noel's four children were recorded (checked all surnames and checked again). Maybe a doctor might have discovered something suspicious and Noel couldn't risk that. Now I might sound disingenuous, because I am, but having researched so many murder cases (more Kent books currently in the planning) one thing I do know for sure, the partners of most murderers can only be described as bloody simple minded and thick. It would be easy for a confident over bearing man like Noel, a butcher, hardened to killing live animals, to suffocate a newborn baby with a pillow whilst his wife slept and then tell the grieving trusting woman it had died in it's sleep and not to worry her pretty head as he would deal with everything - and then just dispose of the corpses himself by some means too horrible to contemplate in his slaughter house. No friend or neighbour would think to question the babies deaths upon seeing a tearful mum in black who was convinced her husband had made all the appropriate arrangements whilst she was still laid up in bed, and let's be honest who would enquire anyway, a neighbour who had seen the pregnant lady, a family member informed of the sad loss by post? If someone told me their baby had died I would feel sorry for them, I certainly wouldn't demand to see the death certificate or start quizzing them. He probably just said as the baby was not baptised the church wouldn't bury it so he had paid for a burial in a public cemetery somewhere. "No, best not see the grave Dear, it will only upset you, let our baby rest in peace." Believe me, I've heard men manipulating women so many times in my prison work. The thick women soaking up their boyfriends lies like gravy, I used to walk away shaking my head. "You know me love, you know I'd never touch a kid, Jesus Christ, the cops have set me up, obviously you don't love me as much as I love you babe. Could you just sneak me in some.... next time you visit ...bla bla bla."

There will always be stupid people and wicked people to manipulate them.

William Noel was a wicked devil. He twisted the police up in knots and made them look ridiculous in court. He continued to lead a charmed life not dying until 1938 when he was 88 years old...Of course these are my own opinions on this case, you may feel that Noel was an angel, totally innocent of his wife's murder, the deaths of all four of his "known" children being just bad luck and he, in his grief, simply forgot to register their deaths every time.

I'm convinced Noel was a serial killing psychopathic bastard who should have danced the Maidstone jig.

Family research:

William Noel born 1850 Hampton Wick Middlesex. Parents were Benjamin Noel and Jane Thatcher. Noel died in 1938.

Sarah Dinah Noel nee Saunders born 1840 Middlesex.

Parents Edward R. and Elizabeth A. Saunders. Died 1893.

Odd they were both from Middlesex yet met in Portsmouth.

Winifred Gibbs born 1860 Leamington Warwickshire. Parents Richard and Emma Caroline Gibbs.

Strangely I couldn't find out when or how Winnie died.

4 children, names unknown, births and deaths all unrecorded.

Sources; were Ancestry.com and the British Newspaper Archive where there are literally dozens of newspapers that covered this case.

18.

The Broadstairs Parcel Bomb 1893

The postman delivered a small parcel to 2 Park Road Broadstairs on the morning of 22nd July 1893. It was addressed to Mr Richard Richards at Oscar Rd, but the postman knew the family had just moved from there to Park Road. The parcel had been redirected from a firm of London solicitors. Messrs C.A.Russ. Who had received it on the day previous.

Mrs Katherine Richards did not like the look of the parcel. It was only 4½ x 3½ inches, very heavy and wrapped in greasy brown paper that smelled of lard. The postmark was W.C.D.O and the stamp 5½d. Although there had been an attempt to disguise the handwriting, perhaps with a shaky left hand, Mr Richards declared to his wife the writing of the original solicitors address was that of his brother William's hand.

The firm of solicitors had recently acted for Richard Richards in a suit against his brother William Mark Richards and had won the case for £1,287 in respect of a joint property purchase that they had fallen out over. The two brothers were now bitter enemies and William had just started a counter claim against Richard for several hundred pounds. William had written several angry letters to Richard via the solicitor and so his handwriting was familiar to both Richard and Katherine. William did not know of his brother's address in Broadstairs which was why (they suspected) he was sending mail via the solicitor's offices.

Katherine, who was German, begged her husband not to open the parcel as she feared it would contain something nasty. Richard shook it a few times and examined it and didn't fancy the look of it either.

Richard was a wealthy property speculator who had resided in Broadstairs off and on for a few years. Currently he was having a property built opposite Broadstairs railway station as a Coffee House. He expected to find a tenant easily and had employed a builder named Mr C Martin to do the construction work. Richard now decided to go and ask Martin's opinion of the little parcel. Katherine and the couple's two small children accompanied Richard into town and found Martin outside by the builder's scaffolding. Jokingly Richard offered Martin the parcel saying "Here you are, I've bought you a present" Martin jokingly replied with something along the lines of "Oh you shouldn't have" Richard then asked Martin what he thought of the parcel and Martin declared that he didn't like the look of it and he handed it back. Both men considered there was only one answer to the problem, open the damned thing.

"Oh God please don't" begged Katherine but Richard already had his pen knife open. Holding the box in his left hand he cut the string pulling it from the wrapper. The immediate explosion was so strong it threw Richards and Martin across the pavement. Katherine's screams brought the public running from all directions. She was flat on her back hugging her children but seemed unharmed physically. Mr Martin's face was covered in blood, he was shaky and shocked but he was able to get up. Mr Richards was not so lucky. His injuries were traumatic. He had taken the full force of the bomb. Half his face had been blown away. His left ear was missing and so was his left hand, but the worst injury was to his stomach which was ripped open and embedded with shrapnel.

A doctor quickly ran to assist and applied a tourniquet to the arm with the severed hand. A horse drawn ambulance raced to get Richard to the Seaman's infirmary. Mr Martin the builder was taken to the doctor's surgery where he had splinters removed from his face and was then allowed home, although he was partially blinded by the flash for many weeks.

Mrs Richards was taken home and her own doctor attended her there for shock. Luckily neither her nor the children were physically harmed. Later that same day Mr Richards died at the hospital. His wounds were severe, his stomach and kidneys were lacerated beyond help. Until the end he had been in extreme agony. He managed to speak only once in his delirium, "Oh Lord what has come upon me?"

An inquest was held for Mr Richards. Katherine was adamant William had sent the parcel bomb, which she called that 'infernal machine'. William Mark Richards, the brother who lived in London, denied everything when questioned by the police. As there was no proof discovered that he had either constructed or sent the parcel bomb to his brother the police had no evidence to arrest him. (No one thought to compare his handwriting to any remains of the bomb wrapper?)

An expert who looked at the fragments of the bomb declared it must have been gunpowder in a tin encased with a plywood box This powder had somehow been ignited by the pulling out of the string that tied up the wrapping paper. (Definitely an expert then)

The verdict was declared wilful murder by person/persons unknown. The case remains officially unsolved but I think it's obvious who the murderer was.

Family Search:

Richard Richards born 1843 in St Columb, Cornwall England.

Wife Katherine Frances (surname unknown) born c1860 Speyer in Rhine, Germany according to census returns.

Richard Richards was buried at St Peter's Broadstairs 26th July 1893.

Children: Supposedly two boys but I could only find one girl: Frances Marguerite Richards born to the couple in 1887.

Sources: Thanet Advertiser 29 July 1893. Whitstable Times 29 July 1893. Manchester Times 28 July 1893. Lloyd's Weekly 30 July 1893. St James Gazette 24 July 1893. Lloyd's Weekly 30 July 1893. St James's Gazette 24 July 1893. Illustrated Police News 29 July 1893 & Ancestry.com

19.

Suicide. Are you Joking? 1893

When you're hurrying along on a freezing winter's day, the last thing you expect to find is a lady lying on top of a manure heap with her head hanging off!

I wish I could say that I eventually solved this bizarre case. Sadly, at the time of writing, I can not. Perhaps you, the reader, may well be holding the answer to this mystery somewhere in your own family history. Did any of your Great Aunts disappear suddenly in 1893?

The grisly discovery was made by a farm labourer in a Garlinge country lane on Saturday the 7th of January 1893.

On Tues 9th of January, the Dover coroner held an inquest at Garlinge in Margate. Quite seriously, he concluded the woman had obviously committed suicide. His only concern, who was she? A description of the lady was placed in the illustrated police news in the hope that someone would be able to identify the body. She was described thus: 40-45 years, 5 feet, 4 inches. Light brown hair - greying. Light blue eyes. Single (no wedding ring) Dressed in an elegant black gown with two rows of velvet at the bottom. She had a black bonnet and a fur lined black cloak faced with beaver fur. (Was the bonnet off or on?)

Beside her body was a brown seal skin handbag, within which, money of £1.3s.4d (a decent sum) was found along with two pairs of ladies gloves and a linen handkerchief.

Next to the dead woman was found a bloodied man's razor. All laundry labels had been cut from her clothing including the hanky. Only a single piece of a label on her under garments retained a partial name – Chapman. No-one could remember seeing the woman around the village. No-one passed the woman on any of the roads leading to Garlinge. She had seemingly materialised out of thin air. The head of this well dressed Jane Doe was completely severed and was barely attached to the back of her neck. She had been all but beheaded. Most strange of all, she was found on top of a stinking heap of animal manure - Naturally this was all clear evidence she had killed herself.

If she was not known in the village, and nobody claimed to have driven the lady to Garlinge or knew of her in Margate, then we are expected to believe she had walked to this rural place, finding her own way there without being seen. She chose to do this in the depth of winter on a freezing cold January morning or during the previous night, if not by road then across the muddy fields. (Were her boots thick with mud?) Having dressed in warm elegant clothing she had left home with a hanky, two pairs of gloves, plenty of money ...and a man's razor in her bag. Then having decided that, yes, this rural lane in Garlinge village was definitely the place where she wanted to end her life, she then chose, not to sit down on the grass, or lean against a tree, but instead to clamber up onto a stinking manure heap. Once seated, savouring the aroma beneath her, she then took off her gloves and put them in her bag. Then taking out the razor, she proceeded to cut her own head off.

What would the fictional Holmes have made of the coroner's verdict? Laughed his deerstalker off probably. My guess is, she was more probably a married man's mistress. She had been lured to the nearby town, Margate, by train, on the pretence of meeting her lover. (Hence the money and spare gloves for the trip) Somewhere she was murdered, probably strangled. Her identity was then striped from her clothing. Her body was then driven by coach to this out of the way rural lane, during the night, by the murderer, who did know the area. The corpse's throat was then slit by the man with some force to disguise the evidence of strangulation, and suggest suicide instead. The body was then thrown from the coach landing by chance on-top of a manure heap by the roadside. Her bag and the razor then thrown down next to her. Perhaps she had threatened to tell the man's wife of the relationship?

Obviously this is only my, extremely fanciful, suggestion of possible events. Had she been a local woman, maybe a destitute labourer's widow, or unmarried pregnant servant girl, then I would still be suspicious of her choosing a smelly old manure heap as the place to end her life and her astonishing ability to keep slicing her own neck until she had almost severed her own head. But perhaps you agree with the coroner?

Sources: Whitstable Times and Herne Bay Herald 14 January 1893. Illustrated Police News 14 Jan 1893. Reynold's Newspaper 8 January 1893.

D J Birkin

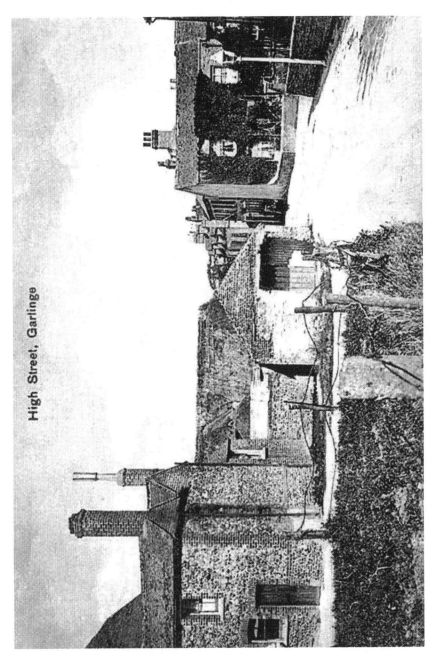

High Street, Garlinge

20.

Slaughter of the Garlinge Babies 1894

Some murders are overly horrific, some just terribly sad, this is an account of two murders that were certainly both.

In 1888, at 154 Crow Hill Garlinge, near Margate, Mrs Jemima Tucker died of an undisclosed illness. She was 53 and had been married to a local bricklayer named William Cornwall Tucker. The marriage had lasted 23 years. Jemima was nine years older than her husband and they had been unable to have children. There was nothing suspicious about her death.

William was now a widower and only 44. He had time to start over and find a new life for himself, perhaps even have the chance of a few children.

By 1891, William Tucker had acquired a new lady love. How long he had known her previously we don't know. Her name was Sarah (surname unknown) and newspaper accounts indicate she may have originated from Hull on the Yorkshire coast.

William and Sarah soon set up house together in Garlinge High Street in an old four room wooden cottage in the delightfully named Happy Valley cottages. The row once stood close to the rear of the Hussar public house.

On all accounts William was the older partner this time, nearly twenty years older than his new young wife. Despite the age difference it appeared to be a love match as the couple were extremely attached to one another. Whether they actually did marry is doubtful as no record could be found, but when Sarah arrived in the village she was already calling herself Mrs Tucker.

In January 1892 William's first child was finally born, a healthy son named after his proud father. The following year, in July 1893, Sarah was pregnant again when, suddenly, out of blue, tragedy struck the new family. William Tucker was taken ill and died. (It may have been typhoid as there were recorded outbreaks of it in Thanet around this time) The pregnant Sarah was grief stricken. How would she manage alone with a baby son and another on the way, without her beloved husband William.

Sarah applied to the parish council for relief and was given a small allowance. The house agent, a Mr G.W Hobbs, collected the rent on behalf of the estate of a lately deceased Mr Townes. Mr Hobbs seems to have been a good and kind man. He was able to sort out a life insurance policy that William Tucker had paid into, plus a small insurance payout from the bricklayers union. Mr Hobbs agreed to be the administer of these funds for Sarah. This meant she would have a small, but manageable income provided in weekly allotments. As soon as the local parish heard of this, they demanded repayment of the meagre sum they had allowed Sarah. She was now reduced to an income of just 13 shillings a week, 3 shillings of which Mr Hobbs had to take back for her weekly rent. Once the insurance money dried up, poor Sarah would have no income at all. This is known to have prayed on her mind adding to her mental anxiety.

In Jan 1894 Sarah's second baby finally arrived. Another healthy boy. Born posthumously, she named him George Cornwall Tucker. Sadly the birth only pushed Sarah closer to the edge of her sanity. Sarah began imagining the neighbours were whispering behind her back, accusing her of murdering her husband, calling her babies nothing but cats! Within a couple of weeks the local doctor decided Sarah was in breakdown and admitted her into the Margate cottage hospital to be rested and assessed for her ability to cope. Arrangement was made for the babies to be temporarily looked after to give Sarah time to recover. She didn't stay long. On 16th February she returned home and collected her children.

William Tucker had come from a large family at Littlebourne near Canterbury. Of his many siblings, at least ten, Thomas Charles Tucker (sometimes calling himself John) was seven years his brother William's junior. He had heard of his sister-in-law's plight and presented himself at her door on her return from hospital in February. (Sarah had been widowed seven months and he hadn't bothered before) Thomas Tucker was a house painter by trade, was sometimes employed, and immediately offered to lodge with Sarah in order to provide her with a little rent money. His reputation appeared a little shady. It was thought locally that Thomas was more likely trying to weasel his way into Sarah's bed in an attempt to avail himself of what little money she had, rather than to help the poor woman.

Neighbours in the past involved themselves in each other's lives far more than they do today. It was not from sheer nosiness or lack of entertainment, but out of a genuine heartfelt community spirit, real concern for their fellow humans. Life was a living soap opera and you never knew when you might need to call on a friend for help yourself.

It was getting on for 10.30am on Tues March the 20th, and Sarah's neighbour, Mrs Emma Sayers, was getting concerned. The walls between the wooden cottages were quite thin. Mrs Sayers was used to hearing Sarah moving about very early in the mornings, walking up and down on the wooden floors, the children giggling or crying, but that day there was only silence. It was much too quiet for Mrs Sayer's liking. She had actually seen Sarah, very early that morning around 6.30am, going into her garden for a fleeting moment to fetch something. Mrs Sayers had expected to see her appear again later as Sarah usually had baby's washing to peg out. But there had been no sign of her and the silence was now deafening Mrs Sayers.

This neighbour was what I often call a 'curtain twitcher' and they make excellent witnesses. If Sarah had gone out, Emma Sayers would not only have seen her, she would have noted the time. Nevertheless, she was genuinely concerned, she was sure that something bad had happened and decided to consult Mr Hobbs, their landlord for advice. (Can you imagine going to your landlord today and saying I haven't seen my neighbour for a few hour. She's too quiet.)

Kind Mr Hobbs came round anyway and finding there was no answer to be had at Sarah's front door he then borrowed a ladder and put it up to the front bedroom window and peered in. Sarah was in, she was half sitting, half lying on the bed. She wasn't moving. He tapped the glass and she still didn't move. The two babies appeared to be asleep next to her but he couldn't see properly. Mr Hobbs climbed over into the back garden and found the back door unlocked. He called out to Sarah and received no answer. Wary of going up to Sarah's bedroom alone, he let in Mrs Sayers and asked her to go up and see if Sarah was alright, she might just be asleep and be shocked if a man walked in on her.

Mrs Sayers was frightened, she agreed, but only if Mr Hobbs was right behind her. So up the stairs they went. The bedroom door was shut, so Mrs Sayers gently knocked and called out, "Mrs Tucker, Mrs Tucker. What is the matter with you?" The reply came in a low hushed voice. "I have murdered my children." Poor Mrs Sayers must have nearly lost her bladder. She and Hobbs raced out of the house to fetch help.

Soon a Mr Marsh, a Mr Dunk the gardener at the Hussar Inn and the baker's wife Mrs Goatham were in the house. Hobbs and Dunk entered the bedroom first and immediately baulked at the terrible scene that met their eyes. There was blood everywhere. The bed clothes were smeared in blood, it was on the floor and splashed up the walls. The babies' heads had been smashed in and their brain matter was popped out and bits of it were also flicked across the bed clothes and up the walls. The two small kiddies were clearly stone dead.

Sarah had a cord around her neck and had tied her own throat to the bedpost. She had multiple wounds on her face and was covered in blood. Poor Mrs Goatham began screaming. Her husband, the Garlinge baker, who was eating in the kitchen of their house, which was behind Sarah's house, heard his wife's screams and rushed to the scene. Mr Goatham quickly cut the cord from Sarah's neck (obviously the other men hadn't bothered) and asked her why she had done such a thing. Sarah's dazed and quiet reply was simply " I don't know."

Mr Dunk had a horse and now set off for Margate town to fetch the doctor. Calling at the police station on the way he was informed that the Garlinge constable was also in Margate that day. Neither the less, Mr Dunk eventually found them both, and with all speed they were soon in attendance. During their absence, Mr Kennet, landlord of the Hussar Inn, had been called to administer any medical help that he could. Mr Kennet was a member of the St John ambulance society. He bathed the wounds on Sarah's face but could do nothing for the children. He thought they had been dead for several hours at least. An old thatcher's bill hook lay on the bedroom floor. Covered in blood and hair, it was obviously the weapon that Sarah had used. After killing her babies, Sarah had then repeatedly smashed herself in the face with the bill hook.

Dr White asked Sarah if she knew where she was, and if she recognised him as her doctor. Sarah seemed unsure. When he mentioned the children Sarah just stared at their little corpses blankly, without any emotion, as if she didn't recognise them at all.

Mr Troughton and Mr Phillipott, also of the St John's ambulance society, were then asked to transport Sarah and the Doctor in a carriage to the Margate cottage hospital.

When later that afternoon she was examined again by Dr White, Sarah appeared not to know anyone and begged that somebody would go and look after her children and feed her cats and dog. In reality she had no pets, and also seemed completely unaware that her children were dead.

An inquest into the deaths of the two baby boys was held the next day at the Hussar inn, the whole village packed in to listen. The brother-in-law, Thomas Tucker, gave evidence that he had left for work around 6am on the day of the tragedy. Before leaving he had gone into Sarah's bedroom to talk to her. She was sitting up in bed with her children beside her. He said she seemed fairly cheerful, more than she had been of late. He asked her if she would bring the babies in their perambulator that evening to meet him near the sea bathing hospital on the front. (beach front at Margate) Sarah had agreed and both boys had been fine when he left. The previous day,

Monday, he said, Sarah had been very depressed and begged him to not leave her alone, so he had taken the day off work and stayed home with her for her sake. Sarah, so Thomas claimed, begged him to get her some stuff (poison) so that she might take it and not be hanged for she didn't know what she might do. Thomas didn't get her any poison, instead he took the eldest child, William, for a walk that evening and mentioned to Mr Hobbs that something should be done for Sarah. Thomas said, on the day of the tragedy he had got news at work, about 2pm, that an incident had happened, and went straight away to the hospital. Sarah asked him to go home and feed her poor (imaginary) cats and dog and was upset that she had lost something, but couldn't remember what it was. Thomas said he returned to see Sarah again, later that afternoon, and she didn't know him. When asked by the coroner if there was any truth to the rumours abounding that Thomas had been taking Sarah's money, he replied certainly not. After which Mr Hobbs gave his account of finding Sarah and the children. Mr Hobbs stated that he had indeed spoken to Thomas Tucker the previous day about Sarah and Tucker had asked for Sarah's weekly allowance to be paid directly over to him. Mr Hobbs had refused Tucker's request.

All witnesses gave their accounts as to Sarah's state of mind and to their finding of her on the day of the tragedy. Dr White gave a long and detailed account of the injuries the children had sustained and estimated they had been dead for about four hours when found. It would appear then, that soon after Thomas had left for work, Sarah had gone to the garden for the bill hook and that is when she had done the deed.

The verdict of the court was that Sarah had murdered both of her children, but was insane and not responsible for her actions at the time. She was later removed from hospital, when physically mended, to Canterbury gaol to await trial for the two counts of murder. At her trial on May 20th, several doctors were called who had examined Sarah Tucker, including the doctor of Barming mental asylum at Maidstone. All gave evidence that Sarah was completely insane and unfit to plead. She was taken back to Canterbury gaol while the home office made a decision as to what to do with her. (Presumably she was sent to a secure asylum) No further news was made public as to what became of Sarah Tucker. The children were buried in Garlinge churchyard.

Some notes on the Tucker family history: No family could be traced for Sarah. Her life before meeting William, even her maiden name remains a mystery at the time of writing this account. No record of a marriage between this William Tucker and any woman named Sarah was found in the national registry for the period between his previous wife's death and his own, suggesting the couple were never actually married.

William Cornwall Tucker was born at Ickham Canterbury in 1844. His parents were Edmund Tucker and his wife Mary Ann Cornwall. Edmund Tucker was a sawyer and carpenter. The family moved several times, mostly settling in and around Littlebourne. Their 11 children found in various census returns were. Edmund 1837, Jane 1839, Albert 1842, William Cornwall 1844, George 1846, Mary 1849. Thomas Charles (John) 1851, Edward 1853, Elizabeth 1855, Sarah 1860 and Emma 1862.

The Hussar pub at Garlinge is still trading. (as of 2020) The Happy Valley cottages were demolished long ago.

What became of Thomas Tucker (sometimes called John) ? Who knows. Presumably he sloped off to find cheap lodgings elsewhere with a widow he could tap for cash.

Sources: The Thanet Advertiser March 24 1894. The Whitstable Times and Herne Bay Herald March 31 1894. Plus various news articles from the British newspaper archives plus personal family search in the IGI and Ancestry.com.

The Hussar Hotel, Garlinge. (postcard author collection)

Mr Goatham's Bakers Cart at Garlinge with son (author)

21.

The Baby in the Locked Tin Box 1895

Caroline Emily Marsh, 19, was tried for the wilful murder of her male infant bastard before Sir Lewis William Cave at the Maidstone assizes on the 12th Jan 1895.

Mr and Mrs Foat, residing at Sea View house Garlinge, deposed that the prisoner was, until arrested, a servant in their employ and had been so for a fortnight. On Dec 12th 1894 Mrs Mary Foat became suspicious of the girl's behaviour. Caroline, who had previously come from Whitfield Dover on the highest of recommendations, confessed to Mrs Foat, when pressed, that she had earlier, at 5.30am, given birth upstairs in her bedroom. When the shocked Mrs Foat asked "Is the baby alive?" Miss Marsh had answered "No, it's in my box, I put my handkerchief around its neck and killed it." She then handed Mrs Foat the key to her tin box. Mrs Foat then asked the girl why she had done such a terrible thing. Caroline had cried and said that she didn't know what she had been doing and begged Mrs Foat not to tell her sweetheart because he was not the child's father, she had gone once with a soldier.

The Foats did not open the box but fetched the constable and witnessed him unlock the box. The dead baby was found under some items of clothing, it still had the hanky tied around its neck, its lips were blue and its tongue was protruding.

PC Whiteman then told the court of his finding of the baby, and added that Miss Marsh was very miserable when he questioned her. She told him she had not intended to kill her baby before it arrived but as soon as it was born it started to cry and she was so afraid Mrs Foat would hear it that she had killed it. She hadn't been in her right mind when she did it. Miss Marsh was then put to bed and the doctor was called.

Dr Robert Thompson confirmed that the girl had indeed just given birth when he examined her. The child, when autopsied, was found to have breathed air before death, therefore it had had an independent life (not still born)

Unusually for this period, the court appeared to have sympathy for Caroline Marsh. Her lawyer called on several persons, including Caroline's Mother, also named Caroline, to give a good account of Miss Marsh, all of whom testified that she was, in their knowledge, a good kind hard working girl who had been in constant employment since she was 14, and would never have done such a thing had she not been in a desperate state, terrified out of her wits from the ordeal of having just given birth all alone. Mr Worsfold Mowll, a Dover solicitor acquainted with the girl's family, gave testimony that the family were most respectable. The girl's father, Henry Marsh, was a farm bailiff at Whitfield Dover employed by the Countess of Guildford. Mr Mowll said he also bore the entire cost of the girl's defence himself! Obviously the Countess was paying and had ordered Mowll to do this on her behalf as she didn't want the scandal of her bailiff being the father of an executed baby murderer.

The judge directed the jury that they should find Miss Marsh guilty of murder *only* if they thought there was evidence that she had deliberately intended to murder the baby and if not then to find her guilty only of concealment of its birth. Despite obvious evidence of deliberate murder, the jury found her guilty only of concealment of a birth because the judge clearly wanted it.

Like Mowll, the judge too obviously wanted to ingratiate himself with the Countess of Guildford.

Caroline Marsh received a prison sentence of just nine months. She was a very lucky girl to have escaped the rope and I think she was also very lucky to have the influence of the Countess of Guildford in her case. After she was released from gaol she went on to have a very long and happy life, marrying and having 12 more children. No doubt her children never knew that their mother was a baby killer.

Family Research: Caroline Emily Marsh Born July 1875 Whitfield Dover Kent. Parents Henry Marsh & Caroline Dixon. Caroline Emily was one of 14 children.

On her release from prison in 1895 she married William Lillywhite (1872-1962) on 20 Oct 1896 at River Church Dover. If he was the sweetheart she had mentioned before, then he was very forgiving of her having another man's baby and murdering it.

Caroline and William had 12 children. Winifred 1897, William 1898, Victor 1901, Irene 1902, Edward 1904, Victoria 1906, Gwendoline 1909,

Hazel 1911, Basil 1914, Myrtle 1916, Lucy 1918 & Clifford in 1920. All the Children lived to a good old age.

Caroline and Lilywhite moved to Storrington in Sussex and then Bletchingley in Surrey where Caroline died in June 1951.

Sources: Canterbury Journal 19 Jan 1895. Morning Post 15 January 1895. Thanet Advertiser 19 January 1895. Ancestry.com.

Caroline Emily Marsh (Lillywhite) in 1917

22.

Thrown off Dumpton Gap 1897

Early on the morning of Sunday 20 June 1897 a girl was found lying unconscious on the beach below Dumpton Gap (between Broadstairs and Ramsgate) having evidently fallen over 60 feet from the cliff top above.

Police Constable Springett of Broadstairs was summoned and found the girl laying almost face down on the sand. Assuming she was dead he rolled her over, whereupon the girl cried out "Oh don't hurt my shoulder" she then told the PC her name was Gertrude Madeline Capel aged 18 of 2 Syndale Place Ramsgate where she lived with her Auntie.

A doctor was immediately summoned and he instructed that the young lady needed to be quickly taken to Ramsgate Seaman's Infirmary. At 8.30am the hospital surgeon examined the girl and found the patient to have fractures of the skull both at the front and the base, a dislocated shoulder and other severe injuries.

The Aunt, Fanny Capel, (a genuine Aunt Fanny) was soon in attendance at her niece's bedside. She explained to the police that Gertie had been in service as a house-maid, who had been 10 months in the employ of Mr & Mrs

Sheppard of 15 Thanet Street (now Rd) Eastcliff. Gertrude had previously lived with her Aunt. When Aunt Fanny asked the question "Gertie, how did it happen?" Gertrude replied "Nothing has happened, I did not like him well enough" Which implied Gertie though she was being asked if she had had sex or been raped. Gertie seemed very confused and her Aunt put the question to her several times to try and get a coherent response from her niece. Gertie then mentioned the name Harry Laslett, then another man, Harold Laslett. Then she said that she had met a man on the cliff and they had gone for a walk together. When asked if she had met the man before, Gertie said, yes, many times. When asked again the man's name Gertie again replied "Harry Laslett." When asked if he lived in Ramsgate, Gertie said she didn't know. She said he had asked if she would be engaged to him, marry him, and she had told him "No, I don't like you enough, I like Harold Goldsmith better." The man then said "You shall not have Harold Goldsmith." Then they quarrelled and the man threw her off the cliff. Gertrude then told the policeman at her bedside that the man came down to the beach and kicked her in the head.

The Nurse in attendance, Florence Farrow, told the Aunt that Gertrude had spoken of it earlier, when first admitted, and had said a man had pushed her off the cliff. She thought the man was named Arthur Lancelot or something like Lancelot and another girl had introduced her to him, but the nurse also thought that Gertie's mind was wandering at the time she had said it.

Gertrude lingered delirious until the Wednesday, before finally slipping into unconsciousness and dying peacefully in the afternoon at 3.15pm.

The police tried to examine the grass on the cliff top and noticed a flattened area where someone could have lain, or struggled, but the public had walked all over the area sightseeing as soon as news had got around of the girl being attacked.

The inquest was held at the Ramsgate Infirmary on Thursday 1 July 1897 before the coroner Dr Hardman of Sandwich. Medical evidence was then given to prove Miss Capel's death resulted from Meningitis of the brain caused by the skull fractures. In addition to this she had dislocated shoulders and severe bruising on her arms and chest that suggested she may have been dragged along. It was also made clear that the body was intact (a virgin) and had not been interfered with. The police under the instruction of Chief Constable Ross and Sergeant Hoare of Broadstairs had sought as many witnesses as possible to try and find an explanation for this bizarre occurrence that had resulted in the death of such an unfortunate young woman.

Robert Phillpot came forward as the witness to discovering Gertrude on the sands. He had been working at the gas works and was walking home along the beach around 4.30am when he had found her. She was a little wet, he recalled, but not soaked, he didn't think the tide had washed over her, just wet from the rain. She was lying about 100 yards towards the Ramsgate side of the Louisa Gateway, about 4 foot out from the base of the cliff, her head facing the sea. Her face was covered in blood. Phillpot thought she was dead so he had gone to find a constable.

Robert Bearne the local coastguard said Dumpton Gap was clear of water at 4.30am and it had been raining a lot there during the night. It seemed that Gertie could not have lain in that spot all night or she would have drowned in the sea.

The lad that Gertie had said she liked, Harold Goldsmith, came forward to say he knew Gertrude Capel and had walked out with her on two occasions but had not seen her since May 24. He was not engaged to her, there was no understanding between them, neither had they ever written to each other.

The police had brought in a young man who's name was Henry Laslett (Harry is usually short for both Harold and Henry) The lad was duly warned and then said he lived at Prospect Cottage Broadstairs. He did know the last witness, Harold Goldsmith, a little, and had viewed Gertrude's body in the mortuary, but he had never seen Gertrude Capel before in his life or ever heard her name. Both he, and his brother Thomas Laslett, then provided detailed alibis for the evening that Gertrude had received her injuries. Thomas Laslett was a married man and expressed his indignation at having his name drawn into the affair. He considered it a slur on his family and was much put out about it. He said both he and his brother had proved to the police with witnesses that they had been at a concert all evening and with friends and family all night. He thought theirs was not the only family in the area by the name Laslett.

Mr Sheppard, Gertie's employer, said that at 5.30 pm on June 19, Gertie had told them she was going out, Mrs Sheppard said "No you can't go out Gertie, you went out on Thursday evening and you are needed here tonight as Mr Sheppard has a guest coming."

Gertrude then went upstairs to her room. At 7pm she came down in her hat and coat and told Mrs Sheppard that she was not stopping any longer and was leaving, she seemed in a temper. Mrs Sheppard said not to leave as she needed Gertie to go on an errand for her, Gertie said "Oh very well, I'll do it and then I'm leaving." Gertie then left to run the errand and returned well before 8pm. She packed her box and said she would send for it. She asked for the remainder of her wages owing, 6 shillings, which she was given. The Sheppards has recently moved to their current smaller house and Gertie had said she would stay with them because she liked Mrs Sheppard. They had tried to get her to stay on Saturday evening but she had insisted on leaving. Gertie then left just after 8pm and they saw her no more. Aunt Fanny confirmed that Gertie was initially going to give up her position when the Sheppard's moved house but had indeed decided to stay on with them at the new house because Mrs Sheppard was so kind to her.

It would appear no one had any idea why Gertie had suddenly decided to quit her job just because she could not go out that night, no one knew of any sweetheart Gertie might have been hoping to meet.

A friend of Gertrude's named Ebenezer Lilliford Miller said he met Gertrude by chance in the High Street at Ramsgate shortly after she had left her employers house about 8.15pm. They chatted and there was talk of Gertie going to Canterbury. Ebenezer then walked with Gertie as far as Granville Gardens. On the way they passed a tall well dressed upper class gent wearing a long duster coat. and Gertie said she was sure he was a friend of hers from London that she had met three weeks previously in Broadstairs. Ebenezer sat on a bench in the gardens with Gertie for a few minutes and then she said she thought she would like to see her friend again so they walked towards the Granville Hotel and parted there at about 8.30pm. He never saw Gertie again.

All witnesses seemed to agree that Gertrude was a happy, cheerful, well balanced and likeable girl with no worries.

There were no other witnesses and the police were determined to try and trace the tall upper class gent in the duster coat. Local boys, like Gertie named, wouldn't have owned a duster coat.

The coroner said it was the most mysterious case that had ever come before him and allowances should be made for the girl's hospital statements as she may have been hysterical after having fallen 60 feet. There was nothing to show where Gertrude had been between the hours of 8.30pm and 4.30am the next morning when she was found on the beach. She had evidently not lain there all night due to the tides or else she would have drowned, so she must have spent the night somewhere.

Men with that kind of violent nature, to go down to the beach and kick her head in, well, they don't change. I doubt that Gertie was his first or last murder.

The verdict was then left open and Gertrude Capel's murder remains unsolved to this day.

Sources: Illustrated Police News 10 July 1897. Whitstable Times and Herne Bay Herald 03 July 1897. Thanet Advertiser 26 June 1897 & other papers in the British newspaper archive.

23.

Failed Murder at Margate 1902

Arthur Robert Bullman, 28, was indicted at Maidstone Spring Assizes 1902 charged with attempting to murder his wife Harriet Elizabeth Bullman.

The couple had married in 1896. Arthur was a ship's carpenter on HMS Cyclops. When he came home on leave to Margate in 1901 Harriet met him and told him she was now living with another man. Arthur later called on her and asked her to walk with him so they could talk about it. He then pulled a pistol from his pocket and shot her. The bullet passed right through her neck. Arthur then attempted to kill himself but only succeeded in shooting himself in the jaw. Both persons were conveyed to hospital for treatment, neither suffered life threatening injuries.

When the police investigated they found Arthur had a letter about him which read;

"I Arthur Bullman of HM Navy do hereby declare and my wife also, to die together, as it is impossible for me to do otherwise under the present surroundings, (I think he meant circumstances) I wish my wife to be buried with me, the world is altogether a stage. (Misquote from As you like it.

Shakespeare fan obviously) Into your hands Lord we commit our spirits." (I would have use commend rather that commit) The Judge was as unimpressed as me, although not so sarky. He sentenced Arthur and his spirit to 12 months with hard labour. Very lenient for attempted murder.

Source: Tamworth Herald 1 March 1902

24.

Attack on Margate Ice Cream Boy 1903

Batista Bernardi was a 17 year old ice cream seller. He spoke very little English but was a popular lad with the Margate residents who were used to seeing him around the streets selling his ices from a hand cart.

In 1903 Batista was attacked in St Lukes Road Margate by a man named Abraham Selvage, alias Abraham Webb, aged 62. Selvage held a grudge against the lad as they had previously boarded at the same house, the landlady of which had thrown Selvage out for causing trouble. He had argued with the lad Batista, thrown fish bones at him and verbally abused Mrs Bonugli the owner of the house. On a previous occasion Selvige had also attacked the boy throwing red powder (ochre) in his face and been bound over by the local magistrates to keep the peace. Abraham Selvage swore in front of witnesses on several occasions that he would now kill Batista.

On June 29th 1903 Selvage dashed out of the shadows in St Lukes Road and grabbed Batista around the neck stabbing the boy in the head several times with a knife before running off up the road. Luckily there were quite a few people around, it being a sunny day, and the lad was quickly bandaged up and taken to a local doctor's house for treatment. The boy had a 3 inch slit on the top of his head. Luckily the knife had skated across his skull and not penetrated it. The doctor stated later that had it been further forward on the forehead it might have proved fatal.

A passing carter named Mr Sayer witnessed the stabbing and set off after Selvage calling out to Richard Griggs, a chimney sweep, "Stop that man he's stabbed a boy" Griggs bravely tackled Selvage who still had the knife in his hand with blood on it. Throwing Selvage on to the back of Sayer's cart a Mr Phillpot joined Griggs in holding him down securely as the horse and cart set off for the police station. Selvage struggled and tried to use the knife against Phillpot but was immediately told by Mr Griggs, a strong gent of 61, that if he didn't desist he would knock him out and dash him from the speeding cart. Once at the police station the policemen recognised Selvage having seen him many times before over the years but was surprised by his current appearance as he had tried to disguise himself by shaving off his normally large bushy beard and wearing a pair of blue tinted glass goggles. (very steampunk)

Abraham Selvage was brought up before the Margate magistrate the next day. All he said in response to the charge against him was " I suppose he isn't dead?" He seemed disappointed when informed that Batista was still alive. Selvige was remanded for trial at the next Maidstone Assizes. The magistrate commended Richard Griggs the chimney sweep for his bravery in apprehending Selvage.

At his trial, Selvage's knife was produced and he was asked why he had carried it. He said he usually carried the knife as he carved small wooden toys and windmills which he hawked around the streets, it was how he made a living.

His only defence was that he had come up from Dover, where he had been recently living, to "Settle with the boy" He had grievances against him and had lost his place in Mrs Bonugli's boarding house because of him. He claimed he meant only to hit him with his hand and somehow the knife must have scratched him.

Abraham Selvage alias Webb was found guilty of deliberately causing bodily harm on the person of Batista Bernardi. He was convicted on his own account and due to there being many witnesses. His having deliberately disguised himself with premeditated intent to commit a crime was also mentioned. He was therefore sentenced to 12 months in Maidstone prison with the recommendation that he be kept to hard labour. The Judge also publicly shamed him as a coward.

Source: Various contemporary accounts in the British Newspaper Archives.

I couldn't find a St Luke's Road in Margate today although the newspapers were very specific. There is a St Lukes Road and a St Lukes Avenue both in Ramsgate

25.

He Blew up his Son with Dynamite 1903

"Do it again and I'll kill you". "Drop dead and go to hell". Jane Henson had been married for 25 years, she'd heard it all before, but just lately her husband, Samuel Henson, had started using a new threat "I'll blow you to hell". Jane never imagined he meant the *blow* part literally.

Samuel Henson was 59, a rough talking, free cursing, common little man. He was barely educated and all he knew was physical labour as a navvy digging canals and roads. Work was in short supply and preference was always given to younger stronger men. Now to find work Sam had to travel the country and be away for weeks on end. When a contract finished he'd be out of work again and penniless. The only real skill he had was using explosives. This often won him employment over the younger men. When Sam was away from home his wife and two grown sons were much happier. Both lads were working. Jane had a part-time job and had also taken on a lodger. They all chipped in to pay the rent and were quite content. Since the Henson's had married they had grown far apart in their expectations of life. Jane aspired to a more comfortable middle age, a few nice clothes and hats, a better class

of friends and a lot less arguments. When Samuel came home he always ruined everything. He objected to her friends, called them snobs, took her money for booze and didn't see why she needed more than one hat. Christmas 1902 became the final straw for Jane. Her friends, local shopkeepers Mr & Mrs Turner, invited both of the Henson's to a 'posh' Christmas party. Jane was really looking forward to going. She dressed up in her finest and the thought of rubbing shoulders with 'Ramsgate's finest' excited her. No sooner had they arrived at the lovely party, Samuel wanted to leave straight away. He'd rather be in the local boozer getting drunk. As an excuse he claimed to be jealous of Jane smiling and chatting with the gentlemen at the party. He said he felt like a fish out of water. And so he embarrassed Jane in front of her friends and made her leave with him. Jane was terribly upset and wouldn't let the matter drop.

WILLIAM HENSON,

Over the next few days they fought like two cats in a sack. Sam accused Jane of going with men behind his back, demanding to know how she'd got the money for her fancy new clothes. Jane told Sam she was leaving him and he threatened to "blow her to kingdom come if she tried it." Jane's sister Emily Long ran a local pub called the Hollicondane Tavern in College Road and now Sam claimed Jane only went there to see her as an excuse to be with other men. The row was the worst they had ever had and the couple were starting to really hate each other.

The Henson's youngest son William John (20) still lived with his parents in Belle Vue Rd Ramsgate, he was a bricklayer and a first class footballer with Ramsgate town team. The Eldest son, Harry, usually lived at home but was away at sea, he was a merchant sailor. The Henson's also had a lodger, William Wells.

(I'll just call him Wells) He was a gardener and Sam didn't seem to have a problem with Wells, probably because he was young and strong and had not the least interest in Jane.

The thing that annoyed Samuel the most was the way everyone took Jane's side all the time.

On the first Monday after Christmas, the 29th Dec 1902, Samuel had to leave for a new job up in Derbyshire. As soon as he left to catch the train Jane packed her belongings and left too. William and Wells went with her.

A few weeks later Samuel came home for the weekend to find his family had moved. He asked around and soon found out where Jane had moved to and expected to stay there himself. As no one was at the new home, he kicked in the door and tore the place apart flinging Jane's clothes and hats around. Samuel then went to the house of Jane's friends, the Turners, at the

Plains of Waterloo, and looked through the window of their house next to their shop.

Jane was in the front parlour with the Turners playing cards so Samuel banged on the glass and yelled "I can see you in there, don't think I can't" Mrs Turner came out and told Sam to go away, his wife didn't wish to see him. Samuel made the usual threats and rumpus before leaving.

Young William had had enough. He said he'd get another house in his name only and he could decide who could and couldn't stay. The three moved to 14 Flora Road Ramsgate. Wells paid his lodging money to William and Harry sent home a portion of his wages. Jane contributed to the housekeeping by working at the Poor Dinner (Help the Aged type place) Wells and William had plenty of work and the house was very comfortable. Everything was glowing rosy until the afternoon of Feb 23rd 1903 when Wells came home to find Samuel in the house.

Jane was at work and William and his father were having a heated conversation about a letter that had arrived from son Harry. Now the letter was actually addressed to Jane and Samuel couldn't read joined up handwriting, but he'd ripped it open and wanted to know what Harry was saying about him and insisted William read it aloud.

Samuel's job had finished and he had nowhere to live. William didn't want his father to stay and it was clear from the letter that Harry didn't want Samuel in the house either. Wells the lodger felt a bit uncomfortable so he made himself something to eat and went down to the local club.

Shortly after 10pm, William popped into the club where Wells was and asked if he'd come home. Jane would be finishing work soon and William feared his Father would turn up again and start on her. The two lads collected Jane from work and all went home together. William was correct,

Samuel was waiting for Jane on the front door step. He had his work bag with him.

Jane didn't want the neighbours to witness a row in the street so Samuel was allowed inside. Once indoors Jane made everyone a bite of supper in the kitchen. The conversation soon got very personal so Wells the lodger took his food upstairs to his room.

Jane popped upstairs for some blankets and informed Wells that as it was late she had told Samuel he could stay the night on the sofa and leave the next morning. As the kitchen was at the back of the house beneath Wells's bedroom, the lodger could hear a bit of the conversation going on below. Samuel wanted to know what arrangements had been made for him to resume living with his family. William and Jane said none had been made and they didn't want him moving back in with them. Wells couldn't hear everything but at one point he did hear Samuel say "So this is to be the end then is it?" and Jane replied "Yes".

What happened next was recalled later by Jane who's memory of events was very hazy. She thought; Samuel got up and went to his coat pocket and took out a cigar. He then put his work bag on the table, opened it, struck a match and lit his cigar and threw the match and cigar into the bag. William realising something was in the bag, maybe an incendiary, grabbed the bag and headed to the adjacent scullery, no doubt intending to douse it in water or throw it into the backyard. As he did so, Samuel grabbed Jane and stabbed her in the neck with a knife making her scream out "Oh Will, come." Jane couldn't remember anything else.

Upstairs, Wells, who's Christian name was also William, thought Jane was screaming for him and so he leaped out of bed. He only got as far as his bedroom door when an enormous explosion ripped through the house.

Choking on the thick dust and fearing the house was now on fire, Wells climbed out the front bedroom window and onto the roof of the window bay below. From there he crossed to the neighbours bay window. The guy next door helped Wells in through his bedroom window and gave him some trousers to put on!

Rear of the house completely demolished

Soon the street was crowded with people thinking there had been a gas explosion. The rear of the neighbouring houses and of those in the street behind were also damaged. Windows up to 300 yards away were blown in.

It was just after midnight when the police and fire brigade quickly appeared on the scene. It was found that there was no fire but the back half of the house was completely demolished. Surely the occupants must all be dead.

Digging through the mountain of bricks that once was the kitchen, the firemen found Jane pinned to the floor with the sofa on top of her, she was still breathing. Samuel was found nearby, unconscious under the rubble, he too was still alive. Their son William unfortunately was not alive. His body was found under the remains of the scullery. All his clothes had been blown off as had his left hand and foot. His body was badly scorched.

An inquest was opened next day (Feb 26th) on the death of William John Henson. This was then adjourned until Jane and Samuel could attend. It would be several weeks before they had recovered enough to attend the inquest.

Jane could remember only bits of the events due to the concussion she had received. Samuel was now sorry that his son had been killed, he had intended they would all died together. He was very angry that Jane had survived, he wished her dead. Samuel said he had purchased Tonite, a form of dynamite, from a friend in Chatham. Lighting the cigar was an excuse to light the fuse in the bag.

Samuel Henson was committed to trial at Maidstone Crown Court on 18th July for the murder of his son and the attempted murder of his wife. He was found guilty and sentenced to be hanged. Whilst awaiting execution he made an half-hearted attempt to slit his own throat. Bizarrely this act compelled the home secretary to see this as an act of remorse and commuted Samuel's sentence to life in prison!

Samuel was eventually declared insane and ended his days in a secure wing for lunatics in a workhouse on the Isle of Wight. Jane on the other hand thrived without her loser husband and lived on in Ramsgate into her 90's.

William Henson was given a huge funeral. His brother Harry came home from sea and all the members of Ramsgate football team attended, as did representatives from other Kent teams. He had been a very well liked young man.

A unique early example of a pictorial floral tribute was ordered by Ramsgate football club. It was a football pitch complete with goal nets. The pitch was made entirely from flowers dyed green.

Sources: Illustrated Police News 07 March 1903, Sheffield Evening Telegraph 26 February 1903, Canterbury Journal 28 February 1903, Thanet Advertiser 28 February 1903, Penny Illustrated Paper 7 March 1903, Thanet Advertiser 25 April 1903, illustrations copyright Evening Express 24th April 1903.

Murder & Foul Deeds Around Margate Ramsgate & Broadstairs

Minster Village, Isle of Thanet 1908 Where Charlotte Turk normally resided

26.

Was Charlotte Turk a Ghost? 1903

Four field workers were pulling Mangelwurzels at Ebbsfleet near Minster Thanet when it came on to rain. The field belonged to Farmer Pearce of nearby Durlock farm.

Wishing to eat their lunch somewhere dry, the field workers made for a pair of derelict cottages in nearby Brook lane. Mr and Mrs Davis, Mr Albert Sylvester and his girlfriend Miss Alice Foster had all used the ruined cottages in the past when working on this farm. They knew how to get in through a window around the back and that once inside they could light a small fire in the old hearth and warm up their tea cans.

Looking in the dirty windows of the first cottage Silvester saw what appeared to be a couple lying on the floor, presumably asleep or making love, so the four workers let themselves into the adjoining cottage. It was a cold wet day and once the two women had warmed up the tea they thought the couple in the other cottage might fancy a cup.

The old walls between the cottages had holes in them so you could climb through from one house into the next. Mrs Davis called out "Will you 'ave a cuppa tea Missus, it'll warm you." but received no answer. Mr

Davis went to have a look and could see someone on the floor, it was just a single person and not a couple as they had previously thought. Silvester and Davis climbed through into the adjoining house to see what was the matter. The person had on a man's jacket and a man's straw boater covering the face, but was wearing a ladies dress the bodice of which was ripped open. Tentatively Silvester lifted the hat. The woman was clearly dead, her face covered in bruises. All four now rushed outside. Silvester ran to tell Farmer Pearce. The two women were very upset, they had not seen the body nor did they want to. The three waited outside for Sylvester to return with help.

Charlotte Turk, maiden name Elgar, was in her 50's and a native of Portsmouth. She had married a Thanet man named William Turk but had split with him over four years previous and had since become an alcoholic. William and Charlotte had both lived as homeless tramps, paying for the occasional nights lodgings but generally sleeping rough. William took farm work where he could find it and Charlotte mainly roamed the streets as a hawker, selling flowers from an arm basket when it suited her, trouble was, as soon as she earned a few pennies she went straight in the nearest pub and got drunk.

Between 1899 and 1903 Charlotte Turk was arrested over twenty times. She became a regular in the newspaper court reports. The magistrates fined and jailed her every time. Drunk and disorderly in Ramsgate 21 days or 15 shillings, same in Canterbury. She never went under arrest quietly either, many times she was carted off to the police cells, sometimes in a wheelbarrow pushed by the coppers! If she had money she would pay the fine, other times she did the porridge. The courts always recommended Charlotte be put in a home for inebriates as she could be a nice woman when sober and was not beyond helping, but there was never an available place to take her in, so out into the street Charlotte would go again only to end up drunk, swearing, fighting and harassing the public.

When the body was found in the empty house, the police took the modern step of having the corpse photographed and asked if the public could identify her. (Sadly the photo no longer seems to exist) As Charlotte was such a familiar figure around Thanet, several policemen came forward to swear the boby was that of Charlotte Turk, as did the matron of Canterbury jail. Davis and Sylvester, the two men who had found the body, said they had met Charlotte in the village before and didn't recognise the body as being her. The two women said the photo was not Charlotte Turk as they had met Mrs Turk several times around minster and that wasn't her.

Eventually William Turk the husband was found. He too said it was not his wife, but admitted he hadn't seen her for three years so she could have changed in that time – not likely. Several locals and publicans swore that the photo *was* definitely the Charlotte Turk they knew.

The coroner was of the opinion that the deceased was therefore Charlotte Turk and she had been beaten to death on Thursday 8th October 1903. The verdict was murder by person/persons unknown - but the jury did add a rider that identity, in their opinion, was still unproven. Nevertheless, the body was buried in Minster churchyard as Charlotte Turk.

A street hawker selling flowers circa 1900
Very much as Charlotte Turk would have looked.

July 29th 1906 was a quiet summer's day. Several Minster villagers were having an afternoon pint in the pub when suddenly a ghost appeared and asked to buy a drink.

News spread like wildfire around the little village with many women nearly frightened out of their wits. A crowd soon gathered to see this apparition. Charlotte Turk had returned from the grave... Naturally the police took the ghost in for questioning.

When asked where she had been for the past three years and why she had not come forward earlier, Charlotte explained that she had mainly been in prison and knew nothing of the affair. It turned out she had been hawking up near Deptford in January 1903, had been arrested, jailed, released and arrested again serving two sentences in Deptford prison. Upon release she had been found a position as a servant, but the position hadn't suited Charlotte and now she had returned to go hawking around her old familiar haunts.

So, who lies in Charlotte Turk's grave? We will probably never know - or who the murderer was.

Strangely I could find no record of death or burial for the real Charlotte Turk....perhaps she really was a ghost.

Sources: Thanet Advertiser for 21 January, 24 June, 11 Nov 1899 and 10 February 1900, 10 October 1903, Irish Times - Monday 30 July 1906. Plus other papers in the British newspaper archives.

27.

Margate Husband Kills Wife 1905

A gas stoker named George Putman, 45, of Victoria Cottages Margate was arrested for the murder of his wife on Sunday 23 April 1902 at the family home.

The eldest daughter of the house, Florence, 16, had called the police. Florrie as she was known, explained that her parents had come home drunk the night previous and slept on the kitchen floor. She later came downstairs when she heard her Mother shout "Stop kicking me George". Florrie tried to stop her father but he turned on her threatening to strike her, the Mother then called out "Don't be a coward George" whereupon her father punch her Mother in the face with a closed fist knocking her to the ground. Florrie, frightened, had run back upstairs. Later George Putman called up the stairs

"Children your Mother is dead, go and get the police".

It was Easter Sunday and the three girls, Florrie, Dora and Maggie were hysterical when the police arrived at the house.

The dead wife was Sophia Jane Putman aged 42. The couple had been fighting because the wife had apparently failed to pay the rent with some money the husband had given her.

The three girls were too distressed to attend the inquest. The charge of murder was reduced to manslaughter. On the 12th July George pleaded not guilty to the charge against him at Maidstone Assizes. It was said the couple were much addicted to drink and the wife's death had occurred from an epileptic fit caused by the husband's blow. George Putman was found guilty of causing his wife's death but not with intent to murder. He received a sentence of only 4 months hard labour.

After note: In November 1905 Henry Putman of Wandsworth, brother of this George Putman, hanged himself. It was thought that insanity was in the family as the father of the two brothers had also previously committed suicide. The three girls were all in domestic service by 1911 living in different houses away from their father. George Putman died in 1914.

I hope those three girls went on to have happier lives after the dreadful childhood they had endured.

Sources: Leeds Mercury 29 April 1905: Kent & Sussex Courier 3 November 1905: Dover Express - Friday 14 July 1905.

28.

Ramsgate Hotel Throat Slashing 1912

At the Bull & George Hotel, High Street, Ramsgate, Tues 29th October 1912, Miss Florence Emma Pickering, 30, was having breakfast. She was a housekeeper and lived in the Hotel.

Suddenly, George Marks, 25, employed as the hotel Boots, rushed into the dinning room and slashed Florence's throat with a razor. The woman's screams attracted a waiter who found Florence on the floor with George standing over her. George then sliced his own throat and fell dead to the floor next to his victim.

An ambulance rushed Florence to hospital. Her life was luckily saved. George Marks had, that very morning, received notice to quit his job. He was engaged to another girl but had become obsessed with Florence since joining the hotel a few months previous. A letter found in his room showed he had been pestering Florence and she had not welcomed his attentions informing him that she could never consider anything other than friendship. Thankfully Florence made a full recovery.

The Bull & George Hotel was destroyed on 17 May 1915 when a Zeppelin bomb gave it a direct hit. Two guests died from injuries. You can watch the incredible real video footage from Pathe News here:
https://www.youtube.com/watch?v=jAKiGpSMRTk

The hotel was demolished afterwards and Ramsgate's first Woolworth's store was built on the site the following year in 1916.

Source: Derby Daily Telegraph 29 Oct 1912:

The New Woolworth Store. Ramsgate 1916

29.

The murder of Sarah Brockman 1914

This really was a squalid little murder. It made me feel quite uneasy. Sometimes you get an instinctive itch that something is wrong with the given facts, that there was something more sinister going on that never came to light. Nothing can be proven now, so if there was a conspiracy of two, we shall never know.

On Wednesday 18th February 1914 Sarah Brockman aged 63, left her home, 24 Seafield Road Ramsgate, at 7.30 pm to nip to the little shop in the next road. Her daughter Alice was due home from work in the next hour and Sarah needed a few groceries. At Mrs Fagg's shop Sarah bought some currants, a few potatoes and half a loaf of bread. Mrs Fagg found her cheerful and watched Sarah go off in the direction of her home.

In the past nobody locked their doors until bedtime and Sarah just pushed opened her front door and entered as usual. Taking her groceries through to the kitchen, Sarah never got as far as putting her string shopping bag on the table before being violently whacked over the head with one of her own kitchen chairs. Such force was used that the chair cracked and fibres from Sarah's black straw hat were embedded into the chair. Her head bled freely as she fell to the kitchen floor. Her assailant now leapt on her, stuffing an apron partially into her mouth and wrapping it around her head. He then further bound her head with a green scarf. Next he tied her hands together with a cord and dragged the unconscious little woman upstairs.

Sarah Brockman's House in Seafield Rd Ramsgate

Throwing her onto her own bed, and as it turned out later, fully aware that she was suffering from severe bronchitis, the attacker left Sarah to suffocate to death while he returned down stairs to await the imminent arrival of Sarah's daughter.

Alice Brockman was 25 and worked as a laundress in Grange Road. It was 8.15pm when Alice arrived home and attempted to open the front door, she was puzzled to find it locked. She called 'Mother' through the letterbox but when no answer came Alice went around to the back yard. She noticed there were no lights on downstairs but the lamp was lit in the back bedroom above her bedroom. The scullery door was open and Alice stepped into the dark room. The instant she did so (*she claimed*) she was landed a hard blow with a strong hand that dashed her to the floor. Sarah's murderer had been laying in wait for Alice. The man was quickly on top of Alice stuffing a hanky into her mouth that tasted of lamp paraffin. A red shawl was then thrown over her face and a cushion placed on top whilst the monster in the dark proceeded to tie her hands together. When her attacker let go his grip to light a lamp, Alice wriggled and shook the cushion and shawl off of her face and was stunned to now recognise her attacker. "Goodness Will, I never thought it was you" said Alice. "Shut up or I'll murder you", (*supposedly*) came the reply from William Hearne Pitcher, he was Alice's own boyfriend.

Pitcher pulled Alice to her feet and told her to get upstairs. Alice refused and asked where her Mother was. "She's gone out" replied Pitcher and with a lamp in his hand he pushed Alice up to her bedroom and onto her bed. Alice now noticed that Pitcher was wearing her stockings over his boots, presumably to quieten his step. He seemed embarrassed that she had noticed and quickly pulled them off.

Reading all the trial accounts that gave every detail of the event and the conversations, I find it odd that Alice never once asked Pitcher why he was doing this, what was he up to, what was he trying to achieve.

Nevertheless Alice now (*claimed*) she said that her brother Fred was expected at any minute. This, apparently seemed to un-nerve Pitcher and he decided they should go back downstairs. (Why go upstairs in the first place?) Once downstairs again Alice asked again about her Mum. "I've killed her" said Pitcher and took Alice back upstairs again to show her. Alice saw her Mother laying across the bottom of her bed in the front bedroom, her head wrapped and covered in clothes.

Now you would have thought Alice would be hysterical at this point and rip the clothes off of her Mother's face to aid her – but no. Pitcher now asked Alice if she would run away with him and she said she would. So Pitcher and Alice both went back down the stairs, *yet again*, this time to run away together (presumably hand in hand skipping.)

This all sounds bizarre to me. No bags being packed, no hysterics over her dead mother, just skipping off together on the spare of the moment?

Pitcher now unlocked the front door and waited for Fred Brockman to arrive? (WHY?) And while he was doing this Alice supposedly ran out the back door.

Sarah Brockman   William Pitcher

She then banged on her neighbours door for help. As she did this Pitcher left the house and called out "Goodnight Alice" and walked off up the road, according to him, to wait. (Wait for what? For Alice to join him as pre-arranged or for the police as he had been told to do?)

The neighbour, Mr Larkin, took Alice in to his wife and then went to fetch the police. When the police arrived by car they found that Sarah Brockman was still a little warm and hadn't been dead long, in fact she may have died after Alice had come home. The inspector sent PC George Champion back to fetch something from the police station. As he went outside to get in the police car, William Pitcher, who was still standing in the street outside, approached him and asked "Has something serious happened?" "Why?" asked the PC. "I'm the man you want" replied Pitcher "I killed the old woman at number 24"

Apparently Pitcher was very calm, appeared to be waiting to talk to the police, showed no evidence of alcohol use and was smoking a cigarette. PC Champion took Pitcher in to inspector Paine where he repeated his confession word for word. He was then arrested and taken away. It's as if Pitcher was following a script and doing exactly what he'd been told to do.

William Pitcher was a bit of an idiot, a simple minded lad of about 20. Alice was 5 or 6 years older. Pitcher was a bricklayer by trade but hadn't worked much. Alice and Pitcher had been courting for two years. He often met her from work and walked her home in the evening. The year previous, Alice's mum had even let him lodge with them for a while, but he never kept a job long and Sarah didn't think he was good enough for her daughter and asked him to move out when he didn't pay her for lodgings. Pitcher then moved to 36 Church Road.

There was a history of mental illness in Pitcher's family according to the chief medical officer at Chartham asylum who was later asked to assess Pitcher's state of mind to see if he was competent enough to stand trial.

Pitcher had several uncles in the asylum on his Father's side of the family and a mentally deficient who sister was also in an asylum. The general opinion of Pitcher was that he was easily led, had an intelligence level well below his age and was mentally unstable.

An inquest was held over two days in February at Ramsgate Town Hall. Pitcher attended and was smartly dressed. He'd been held in Canterbury jail and arrived by train under guard. His parents attended and his mother cried the whole time. Alice gave her version of the events as previously said. Pitcher seemed calm, unconcerned and unexcited by the events until Alice said he had hit her before on other occasions. Pitcher was suddenly very upset by this statement and called out "That's not true Alice, I've never hit you." He then disputed another thing Alice had said by asking "How did I push you upstairs if I was carrying the lamp Alice? You walked up BEHIND me." and "You walked out the front door Alice not run out the back door" When advised not to say anything that might incriminate himself, Pitcher replied. "I will take all the blame then."

I think the last remark is the most telling one of all and appears to have been ignored by the inquest.

The inquest verdict was wilful murder by William Pitcher and he was taken back to Canterbury gaol to await trial.

Sarah Brockman was buried in the St Lawrence end of Ramsgate cemetery, in secret to avoid sightseers. Alice and her brother Fred attended the funeral along with Fred's wife and a crowd of police to keep away any gawpers.

At his trial in June 1914, William Hearne Pitcher admitted murdering Sarah Brockman; he never stated why he had done it.

It also came out that one of Pitcher's own sister's had been attacked in a similar way a few months prior to Sarah Brockman's murder. The sister was a servant and opened the door to the house she worked in only to be overpowered by a man in a hat and mask who threw her to the floor, stuffed a rag in her mouth, tied her hands and spoke of murdering her in a fake weird voice. The man then left her and run off. The police were called and no one was ever apprehended. It seemed likely that Pitcher had 'practised' attacking Sarah on his own sister.

Several doctors gave evidence at the trial that they had examined William Pitcher and it was agreed amongst them that the lad was completely deranged. He was then found guilty of murder but insane. He was sentenced to be held indefinitely at his Majesty's pleasure. That was to be Broadmoor high-security psychiatric hospital in Berkshire.

After the trial, Alice Brockman disappears from public records, obviously she changed her name for fear Pitcher might one day be released.

Pitcher may have been of low intellect and even insane but usually such people do tell the truth as they have not the wit or imagination to invent stories. Personally I feel, from the statements Pitcher made when he was getting stressed out, that Alice was the instigator behind her Mother's murder and she manipulated the idiotic Pitcher to do the deed. Considering the attack on Pitcher's sister was several months previous, and suspecting it was Pitcher that did that. Then the plot to kill Sarah Brockman had been many months in the planning. So who determined that Wednesday the 18th of February was the day to carry out the crime? Because I don't think Pitcher had the intelligence to make a long term plan without being given instructions. Although why Alice should have wanted him to kill off her Mother I couldn't say, maybe she just hated her. Any defence barrister today would tear Alice's story to shreds and soon trick pitcher into telling the whole story.

A possible interesting record might have been set with William Pitcher's incarceration. Contrary to wikipedia's list, Pitcher appears to be the British record holder for the longest sentence ever served in the British prison/secure criminal hospital system. He was sentenced on 22nd June1914 and died in 1975 having served 61 years mostly at Broadmoor. He was buried at Canterbury but it's not clear if that was by family request or whether he was moved to Chartham psychiatric hospital in his twilight years. He was 80 years old. Wikipedia currently maintains that John Straffen held the record for the longest sentence served in the British prison system with 55 years followed by Ian Brady the moors murderer who served 51 years in Broadmoor. Seems that whoever compiled the list had never considered William Hearne Pitcher to see if he was a contender for the record.

Family sources: William Hearne Pitcher was born 8 Oct 1894. His parents were Isaac Hearne Pitcher (1871-1952) and Rosetta Pitcher nee Harris married in 1893. His father was a Furnisher polisher. Isaac and Rosetta had at least 8 children. His Grandfather came to Ramsgate from Surrey and was also named Isaac Hearne Pitcher and was an upholsterer.

William Pitcher's parents lived at 22 Hertford Street Ramsgate.

Alice Brockman was born in St Lawrence Ramsgate in 1889, her brother Fredrick Brockman was also born there (1887-1960)

In 1901 Sarah Brockman's Address was 7 Ashburnham Road Ramsgate. Living there she was calling herself Mary Brockman, a widow, a general shopkeeper trading from home, she stated she was born in London. Alice and Frederick were living with her, both at school and both born in Ramsgate.

In 1911 their Address had changed to 24 Seafield Road Ramsgate. Mrs Brockman was now calling herself Sarah Brockman, was a laundress, a widow, and now claimed she was born at Marlow in Buckinghamshire. Alice and Fredrick were still living with her, both born in Ramsgate. Alice a laundress & Fred a baker. Alice and Frederick's birth registrations stated their father's name was Jesse Brockman & Mother Sarah not Mary. The census returns claimed Sarah, alias Mary Brockman was a widow. In court at her death inquest the daughter Alice stated that her Mother lived apart from her husband and his name was John Brockman – so not dead then and not named Jesse – either Sarah was living a lie (most likely just an unmarried Mother) or she married two men both called Brockman and neither marriage was ever recorded. It also seems odd that Sarah couldn't decide where she had been born. In Feb 1914 son Frederick Brockman was married to Constance Cockerall and lived at 7 Sydney Terrace West Dumpton Lane Ramsgate.

30.

The Dead Baby in the Cupboard 1915

This is a true mystery case, not because the criminal wasn't caught, she was, but because the murderer simply vanished from all records and no one, to this day, has ever been able to discover what happened to her.

At the end of July 1915, a wealthy Italian family, going by the name of Tirracchini, came down to Margate, from London, for a holiday. They brought their servants with them, amongst whom was a nurse named Clemence Descamps and a young cook named Agnes Mary Payne.

On Saturday 27 August nurse Descamps found blood droplets near the lavatory door and quizzed Agnes Payne about them. The nurse had recently suspected that Agnes might be pregnant and had consulted her Mistress about it, but they had then dismissed the idea. The young cook was sitting down and not looking at all well. Nurse Descamps now asked her bluntly where the baby was. Agnes denied nothing, "I've killed it " she said, and then asked the nurse to "put it away or else there would be trouble". She said it was in her room in a cupboard. Nurse Descamps soon found the baby. It was wrapped in an apron and hidden under some clothing. The poor little thing, a girl, had been viciously slashed and stabbed to death with multiple wounds. The attack appeared to have been a very frenzied one with cuts to the baby's face, neck, stomach, arm, chest, legs, thighs and the throat had also been slashed across. Agnes said the child had started crying as soon as it was born and she had killed it to keep It quiet. She handed over the weapon she had used, a kitchen knife. The nurse went and fetched her Master. Mr Vasco Ernesto Tirracchini, her employer, then questioned Agnes a little and seeing that she looked very ill he sent for a doctor and a constable. Detective Sergeant Ashbee cautioned Agnes Payne and then questioned her. Agnes told him she had killed the baby because she was at her wits end and didn't want her Mother to find out about it. She confirmed that the knife was the one she had used. When Dr Ashworth arrived he confirmed that Agnes had just given birth and the child had died from the excessive wounds, blood loss technically being the actual cause of death, the cut to the throat would have been sufficient. He did not question Agnes himself but thought it best to remove her to Minster Cottage Hospital. PC Ashbee accompanied Agnes.

All this information came out at the baby's inquest the next day.

Dr Powell, a medical officer at the Minster Infirmary stated that he had informed Agnes Payne about the inquest, and told her that if she wanted to attend then it could be adjourned until she felt better. Agnes seemed to have had no idea of the trouble she was in and stated that she did not want to attend the inquest. A member of the Jury inquired as to the girl's mental condition but the coroner, Mr Toke-Boys, quite rightly, said that Agnes' mental condition was of no concern to the court as the inquest was just to establish the child's cause of death. The girl's mental health would be considered by others at a later date.

The Jury found a verdict of wilful murder on the child by the Mother Agnes Mary Payne.

And there the story ends. No record has ever been found for her being brought to trial. I searched all newspapers home and abroad for further details and found nothing. I tried every resource I know. I did find out that she had a large family who have descendants today who are also trying to find out what happened to Agnes. I found this case very bizarre. The nurse Clemence Descamps also vanished and has no history at all. And although Mr Tirracchini is recorded as having a telephone in the 1920s and 30s at two Hampstead addresses, he too has no history at all, no relatives worldwide, parents, children, wife (newspaper said he had a wife!) and even his name appears to be completely made up. I tried multiple variations of the spelling. The name Tirracchini, although sounding Italian, has never existed. Judging by his two addresses in Hampstead he was an extremely wealthy man. Did this gent pay to get Agnes put in a private asylum so his name wasn't dragged through a trial and splashed across the London papers? Who was this Italian man calling himself by the made up name Tirracchini? Was he in a wartime protection program under an assumed name? I exhausted all avenues for Agnes Payne, suicide, death, execution, marriage, asylum and workhouse records etc. One of Agnes Payne's family descendants believes Agnes's parents were told that their daughter was put away in a private asylum for life and found out that Agnes already had an illegitimate daughter the year previous (name withheld by family request) and that child had been adopted by a couple unrelated to the Payne family. When the daughter of that adopted daughter later made contact on Ancestry.com it became apparent that she too was equally in the dark as to what had become of her Granny Agnes.

A real mystery then. Here is the date for the one and only newspaper source: Thanet Advertiser 4 Sept 1915.

Family research: Agnes Mary Payne was born in St Pancras London in 1890, she had a twin sister named Florence and lots of siblings all of whom married and had children. She is known to have been in service in Hampstead in 1911 for another family before going to work for the Tirracchini family also in Hampstead. Her parents were George Payne and Esther Brooker. The baby was buried in Margate in August 1915 simply as (Female) Payne.

When the 1921 census for the UK is finally released in 2021 it might be possible to find further clues to the life of the elusive Agnes Payne.

31.

The Chinese Lantern Café 1927

Just the name, The Chinese Lantern Café, sounds so wonderfully evocative of the 1920s. The proprietress of the café was a Mrs Sonia Alexandra Ramsay. She was described as; Charming, veracious, Bohemian in her choice of clothing, youthful with a love of dancing.

In June 1927, in a bedroom above the café, the attractive young Sonia Ramsay lay dead on the floor. A sheet thrown over her head covered the awful spectacle that her brains had been smashed in.

Mrs Ramsay lived at a house called Durlock villa, in Lindenthorpe Rd Broadstairs, with her invalid Husband David Ramsay, her three sons and her Mother Mrs Heilgers. The house was originally the holiday home of the wealthy Mrs Heilgar, a banker's widow, and her daughter's family had only recently moved into it permanently.

Aside from their home Sonia rented a tiny cafe, the Chinese Lantern, a very distinctive café in Harbour Street Broadstairs. The entrance was at the side in a passage named Eldon Place. The exterior was painted bright red with Chinese symbols, the interior hung with gay paper lanterns. Very exotic for the little seaside town in 1927.

The Ramsey family were by no means poor. David Ramsay had good family support and a war pension. Sonia's family were very wealthy, her father had been a partner in the Heilgers family business F. W. Heilgers & Co. known as the Chartered bank of India. Sonia, it seems, had started the café only eighteen months before to give her some occupation, a little life outside of the home.

David Ramsay, an ex-pilot, had been crippled in the first world war. He was described as a brilliant scholar, who had been up at Cambridge and studied law. Due to his permanent injuries he had employed a male nurse named 'Charlie' Robinson, for about four years.

Robinson had, some years prior, worked at a Margate nursing home. That's where he had met Mr Ramsay, he had been his therapy masseur.

Charlie Robinson now worked exclusively for the Ramsay's and had recently moved into the rooms above the café. Apart from attending to Mr Ramsay he had invested a small financial amount in the café, acting as manager when Mrs Ramsay was absent. It was an open secret within the family that Sonia and Robinson were a little more than friendly. In fact Robinson was totally besotted with Sonia and passionate to the point of obsession.

In 1927 it was becoming clear that the café was not paying its own way. There was talk of it having to close if trade didn't pick up. By investing a small amount of cash into the business, Charlie had hoped to keep the business going and maintain his lodgings and thereby continuing his illicit relationship with Sonia. On 30 May 1927, a Tuesday evening, Sonia bid good night to her family in Lindenthorpe Road to go to the café and serve some evening customers. Her Mother, wanting cash for some reason, then went to the café later to cash a cheque and Sonia told her she would return home about 9pm. That was the last time the Mother saw her daughter alive.

Early next morning, finding Sonia had not come home that night, her Mother accompanied by a family friend, a local dairy owner named Charles Rudd, went to the café in search of Sonia. It was they who made the grisly discovery of her battered corpse. The bedroom was in total disarray, furniture and personal items thrown asunder. The body was fully dressed. Downstairs the remains of a meal for two had not been cleared away. Nothing appeared to have been stolen from the café, the only thing missing was Charlie Robinson. The police were immediately alerted and quickly issued a public description of the man they wanted to question. Described as tall, 55ish, greying hair with a grey moustache. Robinson was quite distinctive. He walked with a slight limp, usually in a slouched manner with his hands in his pockets. (Certainly nothing very attractive there for a pretty veracious young woman in her 30's)

The police didn't have long to wait for news of Robinson. Next day, by the North foreland lighthouse at Broadstairs, a man was found rolling in agony under some bushes. His face and hands were blooded and scratched. He appeared to have taken a corrosive substance, and was delirious with pain. Had it not been for the bushes the man would most certainly have rolled off the cliff edge and met his death on the beach far below. A doctor was quickly brought to the scene. He administered an emetic and the man was violently sick. He was then rushed to Ramsgate hospital by motor ambulance. He was identified as Charles Robinson and admitted at 1.40pm. The patient then slipped into a coma. Robinson died at 2.15pm having never regained consciousness. The man who had discovered Robinson was George Ellis, a workman, who later told police that Robinson's head was on a folded coat and he appeared to have laid down in the spot intentionally. It was not a public area and the man would have had to climb two fences to conceal himself in such a dangerous cliff edge position. A bottle of some fluid was gripped in his hand when found and his tie had been torn off in his distress. Ellis & another workman, had been alerted to Robinson's groans from 30-40 yards away.

The Chinese Lantern Cafe is today a Sailing Club

The next day, Friday 3rd June, the inquest into Sonia Ramsay's death was held at Broadstairs Police court. Sonia's mother Mrs Heilgers was in attendance. Dressed in black satin she sat solemnly by the court window, her hands clasped tight in her lap. She was accompanied by two of her other daughters, Louise Heilgers & 'Popsy' (Henrietta) Heilgers, both of whom were minor novelists. The coroner was Mr E T Lambert, with eight jurymen.

First witness was Henry Weymouth a school master of Broadstairs, he had last seen Mrs Ramsay the week previous. He also worked on the council for the collection of rates and had spoken to Sonia about her council liabilities for the café., but said, although friends, she had not confided to him of any troubles. (Seems no point to him having been called) Next witness, local newsagent's wife, Florence Allsworth, said she often held dancing lessons at her home and Mrs Ramsay would attend. Sonia had mentioned Charlie Robinson on several occasions, saying he was her business partner at the café. Mrs Allsworth had last seen Mrs Ramsay on Tuesday 30 May. "She asked me to read her fortune," said Mrs Allsworth. "I told her she would have a violent accident and Mrs Ramsay jokingly replied it would probably be Robinson's fault if she did. She also told me they had been on intimate terms with one another." (Sounds to me like Mrs Allsworth made full use of her public appearance for a bit of creative advertising to launch herself as the town's new mystic Meg. I bet she was in great demand afterwards.)

Mrs Heilger told the inquest she had last seen her daughter, Sonia Ramsay, at the cafe on Tuesday eve (May 30th), Sonia had mentioned that Robinson was in one of his tempers. Two weeks previous he told Mrs Heilger himself that he would kill Sonia if she kept going out dancing. He was known to be extremely jealous of her and wanted her to stay indoors. Mrs Heilger said Robinson took advantage of her son-in-law, Mr Ramsay, because he was an invalid. She did not take Robinson's threat of killing her daughter seriously and neither did Sonia, it was supposed Robinson only said it in hot temper. Mrs Heilger explained that her son-in-law, was painfully aware of his disability and was in full agreement, even encouraged, his young wife to go out dancing. He wanted her to have fun and enjoy her life. "Sonia was a beautiful dancer" sobbed Mrs Heilger. "As light on her feet as a fairy" She told how Robinson had sometimes followed Sonia to dances and caused a scene. Sonia had no wish to be seen out with Robinson in public.

Mrs Heilger then tried to describe the finding of her daughter's murdered body, she spoke so quietly and wretchedly the coroner had to ask her to speak up and repeat her words. She cried "Oh there was blood everywhere" but it was all too much for poor Mrs Heilger and she was allowed to go back to her seat.

As the next witness was Inspector Goldsmith to describe again the finding of Mrs Ramsay's body, it became too much for Mrs Heilger to bear and she was helped from the court by her two daughters.

Inspector Goldman had arrived on the murder scene just before 10.30am. He recalled how he struggled to get the door fully open as Mrs Ramsay's head was behind it. She had a towel around her neck and terrible wounds to her head, she was fully dressed. A bloody hammer was found in a drawer. It was assumed to be the weapon that had been used to inflict the fatal wounds. A pair of men's blood soaked shoes were in the fire grate and a blood soaked suit was in the wardrobe. An eight page letter, smeared in blood, was on the dressing table. Asked if, when found, Robinson had commented on the murder. The inspector replied "no, the man had been too sick to speak when found and went into a coma at the hospital before he died." It then came to light that Charles Robinson was actually John William Robinson. He was a married man with a wife and two grown daughters living and residing in Approach Road Cliftonville Margate, at a house called the Den. It seems that he had suffered a nervous breakdown some time ago and had left his family because of his obsession with Mrs Ramsay. The coroner then read sections from the eight page blooded letter of confession. He thought it would serve no purpose to read it all aloud as it made nasty accusations against several people uninvolved in Mrs Ramsay's death.

"My Dear Wife,

I am afraid I am going to bring a great deal of pain and trouble to you, but it will be the last. For a long time I have been fighting against this terrible depression. I may well tell the truth at last. All though you have been correct in what you say about Mrs Ramsay. I know now that she is the most violent woman on God's Earth."

The letter contained further accusations against Mrs Ramsay, which the coroner declined to read aloud, (but showed to the Jury) before continuing.

"I told her if I found out. I would show her no mercy, I have no fear. I am quite prepared for my long sleep. My body is mine own, I can do what I like with it. Had this woman only been frank with me and told me the truth, that would have been good enough, but it is for her lies and deceit she has paid the penalty."

After further, undisclosed, accusations against Sonia Ramsay the letter ended "You alone have been the best woman on Earth, a good wife and mother, the best wife God ever gave to man and yet I fell.

God bless you all, Dada."

The jury found Sonia Ramsay had been wilfully murder by the now deceased John William Robinson. On Saturday 4th of June an inquest was held again, this time in Ramsgate, on the death of John William

Robinson. The only member of the Robinson family to attend court was Constance Robinson, an adult daughter of the deceased man. She was visibly distressed and faltered in her step. Having viewed her fathers body to confirm identity, she returned to the court and had to be assisted to her seat. The most surprising occurrence was the appearance of a well known London Barrister named Mr Edward Abinger who had been engaged by the Robinson family to represent the deceased!

Various witnesses were called to give evidence of Robinson's behaviour towards Mrs Ramsay, the finding of him at the cliff edge, and medical evidence of his self destruction.

The coroner went over the letter of confession again and asked Constance Robinson a few questions. She replied that she had last seen her father a few weeks previous when he called and asked her to lend him some money. She gave it. It was to invest in the Café. He said he would repay it after Whitsun. She said her Father had left the family some time ago and was prone to outbursts of temper. When asked if she considered her Father to be insane, she replied "no." Mr Abinger then asked Constance some very remarkable questions.

"Did your father's sister murder her two children and commit suicide?" Constance relied quietly "Yes"

"And did your father's brother die in mysterious circumstances?" Constance replied quietly again "Yes, but I was small and don't know anything about it" Mr Abinger then declared that from the wording in the letter of confession, it was clear that Robinson was insane at the time he committed the crime. The verdict of the court was that Robinson committed suicide whilst the balance of his mind was disturbed. So it seems this Mr Abinger had been retained just to make sure that Robinson was confirmed as insane, and that insanity ran in his family. Therefore he wasn't a murdering monster in a jealous love rage, but a poor sick man who didn't know what he was doing. It does seem an unnecessary and expensive step to engage Abinger. It was obvious to all that the man was mentally disturbed.

With the case researched I felt I had still not finished.

Edward Abinger's bizarre questions had me intrigued. I just had to find out who this child murdering sister was. It took an awful lot of detection work to track her down as she had changed her name. The family connection is as follows.

John William Robinson was born in Bentley Warwickshire in 1873. He was the son of Edwin Robinson, a servant coachman and his wife Sarah Rogers. Their other children were: Annie 1865, Joseph 1868, George 1872, Sarah 1876, Elizabeth Laura 1878 & Louise 1879.

John William Robinson (Alias Charlie Robinson) was married to Mary Louisa Watson from Oxfordshire. They had two daughters: Constance Lavinia (The one at the inquest) 1899-1984 & Evelyn Maud in 1907.

In 1901 John & Mary were living in Putney London, he was a mental asylum attendant. In 1911 they had moved to Worthing in Sussex and he was then a Licensed male nurse now calling himself 'Charles Fredrick' for some unknown reason.

So who was the murdering sister? It was the one named Elizabeth Laura Robinson born 1878.

In 1901 Elizabeth was working as a servant in Kensington. Some time later, whilst in London, she became involved with a married man named John Dixon. He was a solicitor, but never practised, he was financially independent. Elizabeth told her parents she was getting married and moving to South Africa. This was a lie. They never left England. Instead, Dixon installed Elizabeth in a Kensington flat as his 'bit on the side.' The relationship continued for quite a few years, producing two sons. Raymond Herbert Dixon in 1908 & Vivien Dixon in 1911. Elizabeth, now calling herself Mrs Dixon, rarely contacted her family again, until in 1914, she wrote to her parents to say she was now widowed. She claimed her husband had been a stockbroker, and had died suddenly in Montreal, Canada. She claimed to be financially provided for. And this appeared to be so, for in 1920 she visited her brother John Robinson (Alias Charlie Robinson) in Margate and splashed out six guineas to rent a house for her holiday. In truth, John Dixon, her lover, had died at home in England attended by his real wife. His solicitor had been instructed to pay his two illegitimate sons the sum of £200. In February 1922, having now spent all of that money, Elizabeth took a flat at Argyll mansions in Chelsea. As her two teenage sons slept in their beds, Elizabeth turned the gas on full in their bedroom and lay down to sleep next to them. All three were discovered dead the next morning. At the inquest, John Robinson, calling himself Charles again, appeared with another of his sisters, Louise Robinson, to give evidence. They stated that they thought their sister Elizabeth was really married and were surprised to hear she wasn't. John Dixon's solicitor explained the truth to the court. The verdict was wilful murder of the two boys by Elizabeth Robinson alias Dixon who had committed suicide.

As to which of John Robinson's brothers had had a mysterious death, I couldn't find out. Neither did I discover why John had assumed the name Charles Fredrick. I suspect his name change may have had something to do with his brother's death and somehow the lawyer Edward Abinger had been involved in that case, which was how Robinson's wife knew of him..

John Robinson's widow, Mary, continued to live at the Den in Cliftonville for several more years, what happened to their two daughters is unknown really except that Constance never married and died in 1984 aged 85.

Heilger Family research:

Sonia Alexandra Heilgers was born in 1891 in India.

The family were of German descent and their surname varied in all records as Heilgers/Helgers/Hilgers and other spellings.

Sonia Heilger Married David Ramsay at Fulham London in 1910. They had three sons. Robert, David & John.

David Ramsay had been born in Argentina in 1888 to British Army parents. He was in London studying as a Law student when he met Sonia in 1910. He was then 22 and she 19. Although crippled during WW1, David lived until 1960 dying at Willesden in Middlesex aged 72.

Today the 'Chinese Lantern Café' is now the clubhouse of the Broadstairs Sailing Club in harbour Street next to the little Palace Cinema.

Sources: Ancestry.com. Shield Daily News June 2 1927. Dover Express 3 June 1927. The Evening New June 3 & 4 1927. Western Daily Press 6 June 1927.Dundee Courier 4 June 1927.Sunday Post 5 June 1927. Illustrated Police News 9 June 1927 Daily Mail 21 Feb 1922 and a large assortment of news articles from the British newspaper archive.

32.

Matricide at the Metropole 1929

Walburga, Lady Paget, was a German Countess who had married the British peer Sir Augustus Berkeley Paget. She became a close friend of Queen Victoria. On 16 Oct 1929 Lady Paget, aged 90, fell asleep by the fire at her home, Unlawater House, Newnham on Severn Gloucester. She woke with a start to find both the newspaper and her skirts aflame. Being frail and unable to rise alone, she rang for her butler Tom Forester who tore the burning clothes off the Lady. She was removed to Charnwood Nursing Home but died the next day from her burns.

A sad tale indeed, but for one reader of the newspaper accounts of poor Lady Paget's death it planted the seed in his mercenary little brain as to how he could commit the perfect murder – or so he thought.

Sidney Harry Fox, 30, booked himself and his mother, Roseline Fox, 63, into the Metropole Hotel in Margate on 17 October 1929. The receptionist thought it odd that neither Mother nor son had any luggage, but Sidney was well spoken and waved off the inquiry, saying they had come from their farm in Hampshire to take the sea air for the benefit of his poor Mother's health and that their luggage was on its way.

Although she was a fat woman, Roseline Fox was in failing health and shook with Parkinson's disease. Her son's attention to his mother and his concern for her every need immediately endeared him to the staff as a loving and devoted son. Sidney made a public display of handing over a large envelope to the receptionist asking if he could take care of it for him in the hotel safe. This gave staff the impression it contained money or valuables of some kind and the couple were not penniless scruffs, which in fact they actually were.

A few days into their stay, and with no luggage materialising, Sidney asked if his Mother might have a warmer room, one with a gas fire, as she was feeling the cold. The ever obliging staff moved Roseline to room 66 with its cosy gas fire and made her comfortable. Roseline had only two shabby dresses and she was wearing both of them. Sidney Fox presented himself as a very amiable young man. He made a point of laughing and chatting with all the hotel staff and was always smartly dressed, although it was noted that he had but one suit of clothes. Nevertheless he kept his suit brushed and sponged and always polished his shoes. On 22 October he asked the staff if they would please keep an eye on his Mother for him as he had to go up to London on business. Once in London Sidney headed for the offices of Cornhill insurance with his Mother's life policy which was due to expire, that day, at noon on the 22nd Oct and asked to extend it by 36 hours to expire at midnight on the 23rd Oct. The policy had been extended several times previously. Sidney explained that he and his Mother were to travel the next day and his mum was worried that she wouldn't be covered in the event of anything bad happening on the journey. The policy was for £2,000 and covered death as well as injury. Sidney paid the extra fee and the policy was duly extended. Sidney then popped along to the Ocean insurance company and arranged a one day policy for £1,000 also to expire at midnight on the 23rd telling them the same story about his Mother travelling. He also tried the Royal and the Sun insurance companies but they refused him. Rather than going straight back to Margate, Sidney spent the night in London with a boyfriend, Sidney was a homosexual. The boyfriend kindly lent him £1 (crafty Fox already had several pounds in his pocket) and in the morning Sidney got the train back to the hotel having spent the borrowed money on a bottle of port and some flowers for his Mother. After going to see Roseline in her room with the gifts he thanked the staff for keeping an eye on her and said "We've just had a sham fight which shows she is feeling better" then said he and Roseline would be leaving the next day.

Roseline Fox & son Sidney Fox
(creative Commons)

After seeing his Mother to bed, Sidney spent time in the hotel bar buying drinks for the band. At 10.40pm he said goodnight and retired to his room. He now had one hour and twenty minutes before his Mother's life insurance was due to expire.

At 11.40pm Sidney appeared on the first floor hotel staircase shouting "Where's the boots, I believe there is a fire, where's the boots, there is a fire and my Mother is up there." (A boots was a male hotel servant, shoe cleaner and general dogs body)

Several people rushed upstairs, amongst them a hotel guest named Samuel Hopkins. The door to room 66 was closed but smoke was seen coming from under the door. Mr Hopkins bravely tied a handkerchief around his face and entered the room on his hands and knees. Finding nothing but a smouldering armchair by the gas fire he dragged it out into the hallway and then re-entered to rescue Roseline who was lying undressed, but for her vest and drawers, across her bed, not in it. Samuel then dragged Roseline out of the smoky room whilst staff threw the armchair out of a window to the pavement below. (Actually a photo proves that the newspaper made up the bit about throwing the chair out just for sensationalism.)

A doctor in the hotel tried to revive Mrs Fox but it was clear she was already dead. Downstairs the hotel manager's wife comforted Sidney cradling the distraught young man's head in her arms. All Sidney could say was "Has the money been found?" He claimed that his Mother had £25 in her handbag and now he believed it was missing. (He never explained why he thought that it was missing because he hadn't been in the room) Bizarrely he then stated that his Mother was a close friend of Walburga, Lady Paget who had recently died in a similar way. (Clearly his inspiration was still fresh in his mind) Everyone at the hotel felt sorry for Sidney, he seemed such a kind devoted son. "Oh my Mummy, my Mummy" he sobbed, although when informed there would have to be an inquest the colour quickly drained from his face as he collapsed to the floor.

Next day an inquest found Roseline Fox had died of suffocation from smoke inhalation on the testimony of the doctor who attended her at the scene. It was an accidental death as she had left newspapers and clothing on an armchair too close to the gas fire, Mrs Fox must've fallen asleep in her underwear (before even getting into bed?).

Sidney now wasted no time in dashing off to a Margate solicitor with the insurance papers. On the strength of them being valid and armed with the inquest verdict, the solicitor advanced Sidney £40 so that he could accompany his Mother's coffin to Norfolk and have her buried in her home village of Great Fransham. (Thus, Fox thought, getting her body far away from Margate) On the morning of 29 Oct Sidney badgered a branch of the Cornhill insurance at Norwich for payment, he

was put off. In the afternoon he buried Roseline. The Cornhill insurance office made inquiries at Margate and became suspicious as the death had occurred on the extension of the policy with literally only minutes to go before it was due to expire, so they decided to contact the police. Sidney had left the Hotel Metropole without paying the bill – Big mistake. The manager of the Metropole, brooding about the fire damage to his hotel and Fox's unpaid bill, opened the fat envelope Fox had deposited in the hotel safe. It contained only scraps of rubbish paper. The manager's wife too was feeling uneasy about Roseline's death. She had comforted Sidney downstairs and yet her hands had reeked of smoke from Sidney's hair. Neither she nor Sidney had been in room 66. The door had been shut when the alarm was raised so how did Sidney come to stink of smoke so strongly when she didn't? The manager and his wife now contacted the police. Several owners of other hotels, in Dover and Folkestone, began contacting the police too. They had seen the photo of Roseline Fox in the newspapers and they also had unpaid accounts against the couple. The police soon found out that Sidney was an undischarged bankrupt. They duly sort him out in Norfolk and arrested him. He faced six charges of obtaining money with forged cheques, by false pretences and for outstanding hotel bills. Add to this the £40 obtained from the Margate solicitor and the convenient almost expired insurance policy claims and Scotland Yard were asked to take a fresh look at Mrs Fox's death.

Detectives now examined room 66, which luckily had been left untouched by the suspicious manager, and noticed that the carpet between the area where the armchair had stood and the gas fire showed no sign of burning, so how had the fire jumped across to the chair? There was a half drunk bottle of port still in the room and a small bottle of petrol. The petrol in itself was not that unusual as many people used it in cigarette lighters and to dab grease spots off of their clothing, but the port was unusual as staff remembered Sidney arriving with it on the night of the fire and Roseline was known to rarely drink more than one small glass.

The home office ordered that the body of Roseline Fox be exhumed from Great Fransham churchyard and delivered to Sir Bernard Spilsbury for autopsy.

Spilsbury, always worth his weight in gold, easily determined that Roseline Fox had been dead before the fire started as there was no smoke in her lungs nor a trace of carbon monoxide in her blood. He also found bruising in the tissues between the larynx and the oesophagus indicating that pressure had been applied to cause suffocation – she had been throttled.

Sidney had been sitting in Maidstone gaol all this time awaiting what he thought was his trial for just forgery and false pretences. He was shocked to be suddenly handcuffed and taken by train to Margate to also be officially charged in Margate Town Hall Court with his Mother's death. Naturally he denied it.

The next home circuit Assizes were to be held at Lewes in Sussex and there Sidney Fox first appeared on 12 March 1930. His trial lasted nine days as 72 witnesses were called to give evidence!

Sidney Fox Arrest Photo - Creative Commons

The prosecution put forward the evidence of the unburned carpet and the insurance policies. They proposed Fox had forcibly plied Roseline with the port to get her very drunk and then strangled the helpless woman leaving her on top of the bed. He then undressed her and set fire to her clothing on the chair and left the room shutting the door to allow a build up of smoke, hoping the fire would spread.

Fox's defence admitted that Sidney was a con-man but said he drew the line at murder. When Sidney Fox was asked if he left hotels without paying the bill? Fox answered "yes." Asked if he found that difficult? Fox answered "No" When asked why he told so many lies, about owning a farm, having been to private college and his father being a wealthy flour mill owner. Fox answered "To impress people" When asked what part he played in rescuing his Mother from the burning room when strangers had risked their lives to help her. Fox replied "None whatsoever"

The latter was the kind of reply jurors dislike. Fox had seen smoke and simply left the door shut knowing his Mother was inside. That didn't seem like the actions of a devoted son or even a normal human being. Fox had made no attempt to rescue Roseline and had not even returned to the room to help after raising the alarm.

Sir Bernard Spilsbury's evidence clinched it. Roseline was murdered and it was game over.

After finding Sidney Fox guilty of the wilful murder of his Mother, matricide, and passing sentence of death by hanging, the court was then lawfully allowed to give out details to the jury and press of Fox's earlier arrest record. He had been a habitual criminal since his teens After having been arrested for stealing at the age of 16, Sid was placed in the Army where he passed forged cheques and in 1917 was sentenced to 3 months for stealing an officer's cheque book, he was then dismissed from the Army. In 1919 he was sentenced to 8 months for forgery. In 1922 he got 15 months for obtaining money with false pretences and in 1924, 6 months for stealing.

On his release, he commenced a bogus affair with a Mrs Morse, who knew nothing of his homosexuality. He stole her jewellery and insured her life for £6000 after which she awoke one night to find the gas-tap full on in her bedroom. Her husband brought a divorce petition naming Fox as co-respondent. Fox was arrested on several charges and imprisoned for 1 year for the jewellery theft in 1928. (It seems Fox had prior murderous intentions) Upon his release from Prison in March 1929 Sidney collected Roseline from Portsmouth infirmary where she had been admitted for illness but also as a distressed homeless pauper unable to look after herself whilst her son had been in prison. Sidney then applied for his Mother's ten shillings a week pension and made her write out a will leaving anything she might have, then or in the future, to him. (He clearly didn't want to share his hoped for insurance payout with his relatives.) The odd couple then travelled all over England staying in hotels, forging cheques and skipping off without paying their accounts. It is most probable that Roseline had no idea what was happening. She was said to be a bit feeble minded and today we would say she had onset dementia. Thankfully the poor woman thought Sidney was just being a wonderful son. Due to the amount of times Sidney had insured his Mother's life and then extended the policies, several expiring altogether. It would appear Fox had planned to Murder Roseline for some time and had simply lost his nerve on previous occasions or couldn't decide how to do it until he read about Lady Paget. Sadly, killing Mummy was probably the only reason he had taken Roseline out of the hospital in the first place.

SYDNEY FOX EXECUTED AT MAIDSTONE GAOL

Warders at Maidstone Prison pinning up the public notice that Fox had been executed

Sidney Harry Fox aged 30 was hanged inside Maidstone gaol on the 8 April 1930 by Albert Pierrepoint. He was the last person ever to be executed at Maidstone Gaol. When the notice was pinned up outside the prison to say the execution had been completed, a crowd of waiting gentlemen, including the national press, raised their hats in approval.

Family Research:

Roseline Rallison baptised 17 June 1866 Great Fransham Norfolk. Daughter of James Rallison and Maria. A sister, Fanny Maria Rallison b1858, married Noah Clarke.

Roseline Rallison married William George Fox 11 July 1866 at Great Fransham Norfolk. She was, first, buried in Great Fransham churchyard on the 29th October 1929, exhumed, then re-buried.

Roseline and William had four Sons:

William Edward George Fox b1888, Reginald Mitchell Fox b1892, Cecil Rallison Fox b1894 & Sidney Harry Fox b1899. Sidney was born in the village of Great Fransham Norfolk.

Her husband William George Fox was born 1866 at Doncaster Yorkshire the son of Mitchell Fox & Mary-Ann Baterbee.

From the census returns it appears Sidney's father was a railway signalman at some point but seems to have deserted the family sometime after 1899 and Roseline & her sons then moved in with her 86 yr father who was described in the census as a pauper, but Roseline was not claiming to be a widow.

Husband William Fox's death is unknown. Sons Reginald & Cecil Fox died in WW1. What became of son William is unknown but he is believed by a few surviving family relatives that he outlived Sidney and changed his name to avoid gossip. The son's occupations were given at various times as Agricultural labourers and bricklayers in the Norfolk area. Roseline and William lived in various regions: Great Fransham & Gressenhall Norfolk & Carlton Colville Suffolk.

Between 1939 and 1945 the Hotel Metropole Margate and surrounding properties were demolished.

St Mary's General hospital Milton Street Portsmouth was known as St Mary's Infirmary 1928-1930 and prior to that as Portsea Island Workhouse.

Sources: Dundee Courier 29 November 1929. Gloucestershire Echo 28 November 1929. Derby Daily Telegraph 14 November 1929. Illustrated police News 6 Feb 1930 & 27 March 1930. Nottingham Evening Post 9 January 1930 & Ancestry.com.

33.

Who Murdered Margery Wren? 1930

With most unsolved murders it is usually pretty obvious who the murderer really was but either it couldn't be proven absolutely at the time, or the judges were just incredibly stupid and misdirected the jury letting the guilty walk free. In this bizarre case however there are so many potential suspects that it was, and still is, more like an Agatha Christie novel, but one that in all probability will remain forever a complete mystery.

It was about 6pm on a Saturday evening in September 1930. Ellen Marvell was about to have her tea when her mum realised she'd run out of custard powder. Ellen, who was 12, lived in Church road Ramsgate opposite a small shop and her mum asked her to nip across and quickly buy a packet. The shop was known locally as the 'Tuck Shop' and was a small general store run by an elderly spinster named Margery Wren. Ellen did as asked but found the shop door locked and so she knocked. Margery Wren unlocked the door and let Ellen in. The girl was alarmed to see Miss Wren's head was bleeding. Still the old lady served her and Ellen ran back across the road to tell her parents that Miss Wren might have had an accident. Immediately Mr Marvell went across to the shop.

Margery said she had just had a bit of a tumble and hit her head on a pair of fire tongs. The tongs were still on the shop floor and had blood on them. The little shop was the front room of a small end of terrace house. The room behind was Miss Wren's living room, then a scullery kitchen was behind that. Upstairs were two bedrooms. Mr Marvell thought it was odd that the back sitting room fire tongs should even be in the shop as the shop room had no working fireplace. An old armchair behind the counter was where Miss Wren usually sat during the day and Mr Marvell now made her sit down. She looked dazed and pale and seemed to be more than just slightly injured. Quickly he sent Ellen round to 7 Chapel Place to fetch Dr Archibald and to tell the doctor to call the police too. When examined, Miss Wren was found to have severe wounds to the back of her head, concussion and suspicious red marks around her neck. The doctor rightly suspected the old lady had not accidentally fallen but had been brutally assaulted with an attempt to strangle her.

Margery was quickly removed to Ramsgate hospital, still insisting she had just tumbled from a step ladder in the shop onto the tongs and it was nothing serious. Margery appeared very frightened and the police didn't believe her story.

The little shop at 2 Church Rd had been owned since 1900 by Margery's older (late) sister Mary Jane Wren who was always known as Jenny. Young people today probably don't know what a farthing was, but it was a tiny coin we once had that was worth a quarter of an old penny. On the coin was a Wren bird, the females are called Jennies. The Wren is the smallest British bird and the farthing was the smallest coin. Naturally any small girl with the surname Wren would get nicknamed Jenny Wren in those days.

The tuck shop was close to St Georges primary school in Church Rd and frequented by all the local children wanting toffees, fruit salads, sherbet and gobstoppers. (The school since demolished)

The Wren's shop was never a profitable business or intended to be so, it was just a retirement home that ticked along and gave Jenny something to do. When Margery retired from service as a housemaid she moved in with Jenny and the two old spinster sisters lived together quite amicably. They didn't have any enemies and were liked by all the neighbours.

Inquiries by the police found that Margery had often told people that she was well off and had plenty of money and even property in London. She was known to have lent money to relatives and talked of having hidden money around the house. The police quite naturally assumed that Miss Wren had been the victim of a local robber so they were very surprised when Margery flatly refused to give a description of her attacker and insisted she had just fallen over.

The Chief Constable of Ramsgate, Mr. S. F. Butler, now sought the help of Scotland yard. He wanted a full search of the premises by professionals and fingerprints taken. Chief Inspector Hambrook and Detective Sergeant Carson were sent down to Ramsgate to take on the case. Small amounts of money, just pennies and shillings and the odd pound note were found in the property as well as the tins of small coins that Miss Wren used behind the counter. There was never a cash register as the shop was run on very old fashioned lines. Unless there had been a large stash of money somewhere previous it seemed that money was not the motive for the crime. So what had the intruder been after? Upstairs the bedrooms had been ransacked with cupboards left open and drawers pulled out. It would seem the villain had been searching for something, maybe documents or jewellery and all this whilst Margery was still downstairs.

Miss Margery Wren

Margery Wren was now very weak and starting to deteriorate fast. She was put into a private room at the hospital and a police presence sat with her around the clock. Every effect was made to cajole her into talking but to no avail. Margery was determined to protect her attacker. Occasionally she would slip into unconsciousness and then awake confused and mutter odd sentences such as: "He tried to borrow money" "I don't know why he should have come into the shop" followed by "Is the little black bag safe ?" and "His face was red and his eyes were glaring" once she mysteriously cried out "You can't take it. Oh, don't."

2 Church Road in 1930

As it looks today, not much of an improvement

The police found the little black bag, it was a handbag, unopened with a few shillings still inside it. The vicar begged Margery to tell all she knew for he feared she might soon die and shouldn't go with it on her conscience. Margery only replied "You say I am dying. Well, that means I am going home. Let him live in his sins." When the vicar left, Margery said to Mrs Baldwin, a friend, who was present, "I didn't tell him anything, see."

With her persistent refusal to talk it suggested to the police that she was either fond of the person or more likely he was a relative or friend and she wished to spare the feelings of the culprit's relations. The police began to bring in the relatives for questioning.

It was variously reported at the time that Margery was 82 when in fact she was 79 having been born in 1851 at Broadstairs. She'd had two sisters and a brother all of whom had predeceased her. The closest relatives she had left were a few elderly cousins and their offspring. When interviewed they were all able to provide alibis but they soon began pointing the finger at each other. One female relative in Gravesend wrote twice to the police naming another relative she was adamant had done the deed. The man in question was found to have visited Margery the very day she had been attacked, but he could prove he had left the scene before 2pm and this was backed up by a neighbour who saw him leave the shop and saw Miss Wren again alive and well after 3pm when she was sweeping the shop doorstep and again she was seen well and uninjured by the coal merchant when he called at approx 5.15pm, the chap in the frame was able to prove he was already miles away by then.

It seemed many relatives were in the habit of stopping by and tapping the old lady for a few quid but none were found to be in dire financial straits or demanding large amounts, usually just a quid or ten bob until pay day.

In terms of distance the closest relatives were only a few roads away. Mrs Hannah Cook, (71) a widow, was Margery's first cousin. Her father Edward Wren had been the brother of Margery's father William Wren. Hannah had seven adult children, several of whom still lived in Ramsgate and had children of their own; they all knew Margery very well. Hannah lived in the now demolished old Montefiore Cottages off Hereson Rd. Most Sunday's Margery would have her dinner round at Hannah's house and afterwards Hannah's son Thomas Cook (47) would walk Margery back home at around 8pm. Thomas was the caretaker at St George's school, actually in Church Road. He saw Margery frequently and was, for a brief while, a suspect. He said he had last seen her in the street on Thursday and refused to believe Margery had even been attacked as she was always tripping over her long skirts and falling down. The alibi he provided checked out. Scotland Yard's fingerprint test proved worthless. The shop was smothered in customer's prints and upstairs the only fresh prints were Margery's. The attacker had most likely worn gloves. One clue, a hanky with blood spots, proved to be an innocent loss by a local child who came forward with his parents to claim it.

The police were getting nowhere without Margery's help. They insisted she made an official statement.

Ramsgate Hospital.

It was now Thursday, Margery had been in hospital four days and was barely conscious much of the time. A doctor insisted on being present whilst the old lady was questioned. She still refused to name her attacker and avoided questions. She was very confused anyway and only mumbled but the police gleaned the additional information that Margery had lent money to relatives in Dover and £10 to a man she named (his name not made public) who was in business in a town near Dover (Folkestone. Deal?) but that was all she would say. They set off to make enquiries anyway and got nowhere.

At 2.30pm on Thursday Sept 23rd Margery died. No relatives were by her bedside. Hannah Cook had visited once during the week, as had the friend Mrs Baldwin, no one else had bothered.

One distant relative turned up at the hospital after Miss Wren had died. He was William Brown, a carpenter from Clapham, who claimed his deceased Mother had been a cousin of Margery's and he had read about her attack in the newspapers and so naturally he had desperately rushed to be with her even taking the express train. Obviously he didn't really rush as he later admitted he had stopped off for some dinner on the way and that's why he had arrived too late to see her alive.

The autopsy was carried out by the famous Sir Bernard Spilsbury who it was felt was the best person to determine if Margery had simply fallen or had really been murdered. He came down to Ramsgate and was assisted by the local Dr Archibald. They confirmed beyond doubt that Margery had been murdered. Apart from being beaten over the head with the tongs there had been a serious attempt to manually throttle her. There were man size fingerprint bruises around her throat. The assailant probably thought he had achieved his aim in killing her at the time.

Now Margery was dead there was an obvious line of enquiry to investigate. Her will. Did she leave one, and if so, who would benefit from wanting poor old Margery dead. It turned out she didn't have a will and didn't have anything to leave anyway. When her sister Jenny Wren had died in 1927 she had left an extensive estate. £921, enough to buy nine houses in Ramsgate at that time! The tuck shop, including its good will, was only valued at £100 and was in Jenny's name only. Margery was allowed to continue living in the shop and trade there to support herself but after her death everything was to go to Jenny's chosen beneficiary. That person turned out to be no other than Dr Richard James Archibald! The very same doctor who had first attended Margery and assisted Spilsbury with her autopsy!

On October 24th, the coroner's inquiry was held.

Dr Archibald appeared to express complete surprise at being informed in court that he was the only beneficiary under the late sister's will, saying he had done Miss Jenny Wren a small service many years ago and afterwards she had become his patient but that is all he knew of her, no more than the man in the moon! He then made the flippant remark that "he soon expected to read in the newspapers that the Doctor is now being questioned!" Sadly he wasn't questioned. The police presumably thought the Doctor was above suspicion. (Personally I don't understand why the doctor was not informed by the executor that he was Jenny Wren's sole heir at the time of her death back in 1927, even if he had to wait for Margery to die in order to get the money, as legally he certainly should have been informed, unless of course the doctor was lying, because anyone mentioned in a will must be notified of such and this disclosure should have rung alarm bells with the court and the police.)

The Coroner in summing up said;

"The reason she (Margery Wren) refused to tell may be assumed to be that she wished to shield someone. I am disposed to attach more importance to the statement made by the dead woman when she was near unconscious than to the statements made when she was in full possession of her senses. In one of these unconscious moments she said, 'You can't take it. Oh, don't.' I want to tell you that there is no evidence on which you could find a verdict against any of the persons referred to in her statements. The fullest inquiries have been made into the circumstances, and if any real evidence had resulted from the inquiries it would have been brought before you." The verdict was the inevitable - Murder by person/persons unknown.

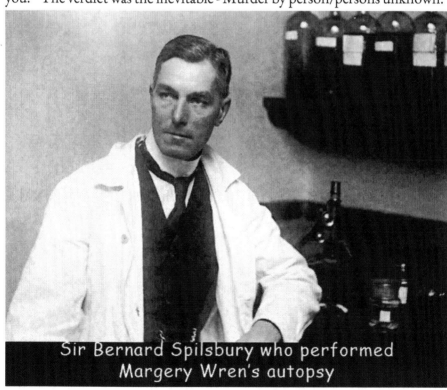

Sir Bernard Spilsbury who performed Margery Wren's autopsy

Another possible suspect, in my view, was also, like Dr Archibald, seen as above suspicion, and that was Hannah Cook's youngest son Arthur. He lived in London and had come home to Ramsgate for a weekend break the same day Margery was attacked. Arthur Cook, 31, was a police constable. He immediately took compassionate leave and stayed on for the funeral. He was the only relative to attend the burial. Would the police have overlooked a fellow copper? Did Arthur believe Margery was stinking rich and thought his family was going to get the lot if she died, had Margery hinted she was leaving them all her money in order to sweeten them up for her free Sunday dinners? A cynical person might say the murderer can usually be found at the graveside of their victim.

There were only three mourners in total anyway, the other two were Mr H. Jarratt, insurance agent of 27 Picton Rd who was one of the executors of the late sister's will (he had nothing really to gain but his fee) and The Chief Constable S. F. Butler. There were only three wreaths. One from the Cook family, one from the Ramsgate Police and one from the aforementioned Mr Jaratt. A public crowd of around 100 sightseers had assembled in Church Road on the day expecting to see the hearse depart from the shop, they were disappointed. The police had arranged for the burial to take place discreetly in the late afternoon with the body going direct from the undertakers. Margery was buried in the same grave as her sister Jenny in Ramsgate cemetery.

The plot in the cemetery is number 613 but today no headstone is present - if there ever was one, but if you can find it do leave the old gal a few flowers.

Rather disgustingly, Dr Archibald didn't bother to attend the funeral or even bother to send a wreath - but he wasted no time in selling the shop immediately at auction for £105 and claiming the rest of his inheritance money which amounted to over £900. Archibald is still top of my list of suspects and I would love to find out why Jenny's two executors, solicitor Stewart Watson Oldshaw and Harry Jarratt, never informed Dr Archibald of his inheritance 2 years before when Jenny's will was proved in 1927 as they were legally obliged to do so as he was the beneficiary.

No one was ever arrested in connection with the death of poor old Margery Wren and the case remains unsolved. Due to the length of time that has passed the police are obviously no longer actively seeking the murderer, whom it may be assumed has since died having got away with their rotten crime.

There are a few possible leads to investigate should any future sleuths want to try their hand at solving this mystery case and therefore I am here adding my two penneth-worth of suggestions.

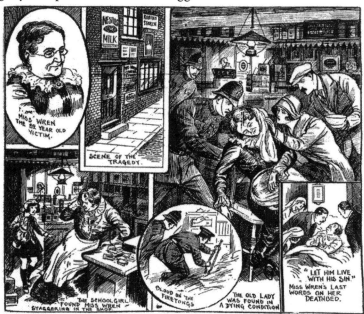

BRUTAL ATTACK ON ELDERLY WOMAN IN A RAMSGATE SHOP

Hannah Cook indicated, according to news reports, that there was a rumour in the family that when the sister Jenny (Mary-Ann) Wren was in service as a cook in London she befriended a girl who had a baby, the girl was unmarried and Jenny may have adopted or taken on the child herself, although no one in the family ever saw it. The father of this unknown, unseen baby paid Jenny 'hush' money. It was just family gossip with no evidence to support it but there is still the begging question to be answered, where did Jenny get all her money from?

Jenny had been in service in London as a cook for most of her adult life until about 50-55 years old when suddenly in January 1900 she inherited the little Ramsgate tuck shop from her Aunt (her Mother's sister Sarah Roughton nee Richards) Immediately Jenny packed in her job and moved to Ramsgate but amazingly she already owned several houses in London that she was renting out. It seems the Aunt was a widow with no children of her own, her husband Henry Roughton had died in 1883 and Sarah had lived on in the shop alone until her own death there in 1900. Jenny was her favourite niece and the sole beneficiary although apart from the scruffy little Ramsgate shop there was no money to speak of. Now, Victorian live-in servants never earned much and certainly could never have saved enough cash to buy a house let alone several. So where did Jenny get the money from to buy the other properties?

Then there is also the obvious original question of what was the attacker looking for that day? If Margery had been bragging that it was her who had all the money, although she had nothing, then might not a close relative want to know if they were in her will? All her relatives when questioned seemed to think Margery was rich, she had told them herself that she owned houses in London. They believed this was a fact and had no idea the properties spoken of had belonged to her deceased sister instead. Everyone assumed the shop was Margery's too. The police even made an appeal for anyone renting or dealing with any property belonging to Margery, and not Jenny, to come forward, no one did, not a tenant, a solicitor or a house agent. The only properties had been those of the sister Jenny and they had all been sold after her death back in 1927 with the funds being invested and don't forget Jarratt was executor of those funds. The fact the attacker was searching for something other than money strongly eliminates a random attack by a stranger. Then there are the words she called out in her delirium; "Don't take it. Oh don't!" That suggests an object that was personal to Margery or maybe a document that she didn't want disclosed because it would show her family in a poor light, an illegitimate child for example?. And who would know of such a thing hidden away except a close relative. Then there is the question of the locked shop door and the order in which the crime was perpetrated. The police seemed to have decided that Miss Wren had been sitting in her shop armchair when she was hit over the head from behind. So that begs the question of how did someone enter the shop door, go past Margery sitting behind her counter and into the back living room to pick up the fire tongs and then come back into the shop and bash her head in from behind?

There are several possibilities to the order of events.

The attacker locked the shop door himself after entering so as not to be disturbed. In which case why didn't Margery just leave the shop when he went upstairs. This could imply that she wasn't frightened and so it wasn't a stranger or she was forced upstairs with him. Or did he try to kill her first and then took his time upstairs ransacking the place. That seems unlikely as a customer could have seen her injured through the window and have raised the alarm with the attacker trapped upstairs. Plus if he didn't find what he wanted upstairs he couldn't ask Margery about it if he'd already killed her, or thought he had. Or did he see Margery dozing in her chair through the shop window and knew to sneak in the back way? There is an entrance in the next street, now blocked, but it once led to the shop yard. The only toilet was in the yard so it is most likely the back door was unlocked at most times. The villain could have sneaked upstairs without Margery knowing and not finding what he wanted, come down, grabbed the tongs, surprised Margery, who was maybe napping, and then bashed her when she wouldn't give him what he wanted, although he would have had to be very quiet at ransacking and very confidant to attempt such a raid.

Maybe he left again by the back door (I would) and that's why no one saw him. But then at what stage did the attacker also attempt to strangle Margery and did that happen whilst she sat in the chair? I suggest that the intruder did get what he came for. He chose a Sunday afternoon knowing it would be quiet with very few customers around - but then how did he know that Margery wasn't having dinner with her cousin that day? He locked the shop door as he entered, confronted Margery as to what he had come for and then forced Margery upstairs to hunt for it, she wouldn't tell him where it was, hence pulling the bedrooms apart, he finally found what he wanted, hence Margery pleading "Don't take it. Oh don't!", then marched her back down stairs. He then made the surprise murderous attack on her just as she thought he was leaving. He then sneaked out of the back door thinking he had left the old gal for dead on the shop floor. Unbeknown to him Margery then roused herself when little Ellen knocked on the door. And if this is a reasonably correct explanation of the timeline of the events then Margery was strangled and bashed in the shop in full view of any passers by then the perpetrator took a huge risk of being seen through the shop window, unless when she initially got knocked down she fell behind the counter out of sight plus the window was obscured somewhat with goods and adverts. And this all took place within a time frame of 30-45 minutes from when the coal man left at approx 5.15pm to when little Ellen found Margery at approx 6pm.

However it was done, it has the smell of an angry personal attack all over it and not the act of a random stranger running in to grab some quick cash from a run down tatty shop.

During my research I discovered a new coincidence, or maybe a clue that should be mentioned here to assist anyone with a taste to investigate further, but take it with a pinch of salt as it's only a gut theory.

It seems that Dr Richard Archibald was born in Aug 1877. His baptism home address was given as 20 Auckland Terrace Battersea London. His father, James Archibald, died of stomach cancer when Richard was only 2 years old. He was estranged from his wife at the time of death and living at 21 Selwood Terrace Kensington. (I ordered his death certificate) When I checked the 1881 census return, Mary-Ann (Jenny) Wren was also living in Kensington at 22 Stanley Crescent although where she was living in 1877 is a mystery as she fails to appear on any 1871 census. James's wife, who registered his death, was still living at 20 Auckland Road Battersea with their children, so the couple were estranged. After James Archibald died the wife, Charlotte Archibald, then moved into the Kensington house with her daughters and the 2 year old Richard. Odd that she should do this and not stay in her own home but then Kensington was upmarket and Battersea was a working class scum. The couple were not wealthy, James was just a clerk and renting two houses, the Kensington one must have been a financial burden. I can only guess that the rent on the Kensington house had been paid in advance and Charlotte made the financial decision to give up the Battersea house as her husband's will left her virtually nothing. Yet Charlotte Archibald never worked and on future census returns she stated that she was financially independent living on her own means – So who was supporting her? Who paid to put her son Richard through medical school? When Charlotte died in 1929 (just before Margery Wren) she left several thousand pounds to her eldest daughter Amelia. When Amelia died in 1941 she left 15k to her sister Edith and nothing to her brother Richard the doctor, not even a keepsake. It seems both sisters had never married, never had to work and had always lived with Mother in financial comfort. Where had their money come from? Why had Dr Richard been left out of this family? If I had to guess I would say that Jenny's family had come close to the truth hinting that there was a mystery baby.

When Richard Archibald grew up and qualified as a doctor one would think he would have wanted to stay in London near his old widowed Mother and his spinster sisters so why did he marry a London girl in 1907 and immediately move away from his and her families down to Ramsgate and end up around the corner from Jenny again? There is a possibility which I think could suggest an answer although I have no proof. Was Jenny herself made pregnant by a married man, perhaps the employer she cooked for. She was 32 years old when Richard Archibald was born. The man then maybe asked his solicitor to find a couple to take the newborn child and the solicitor's own clerk, James Archibald, agreed to take the baby on for a large cash inducement and the baby was registered in his name. This could explain Jenny receiving 'hush' money to set her up for life. How James Archibald, a lowly clerk, was able to suddenly pay the rent on two homes and how Charlotte Archibald, his widow became financially independent for life. Maybe, these are all maybes, maybe Richard's mother eventually told him that he was illegitimate and he tracked down Jenny and moved to Ramsgate in 1907 to be near her and get to know her. Is that why she made her will in his favour? It could then be very possible that Richard discovered he was in Jenny's will and was concerned that the story of his true parentage would come out and the scandal would destroy his career. He would certainly lose his clientele in Ramsgate. No NHS in those days, people paid for doctors. One whiff of a dirty scandal and they'd go elsewhere. His name would be gossiped around any rotary, masonic or gentlemen's clubs. Today we scoff as such ideas but in the past most would turn their backs on an illegitimate doctor in disgust, "He's a bastard don't cha know, bad blood." He was clearly a bit of a snob himself anyway, stating on his marriage certificate that his father was a solicitor when he was only a clerk. And what would his wife and her family think?

It is not implausible that he could have hounded Margery for any paperwork or letters she might have of her sister's, like adoption papers or payments from his real father out of desperation to destroy them. Dr Archibald was the only person with real motive to see Margery dead, not only to silence her but also to hasten his inheritance as I don't believe for a second that he was unaware of it. It would be interesting to know if he and Jaratt were both Masons in the same lodge. I think this could easily be the reason that Margery kept so quiet, she obviously knew what was in her sister's will because it concerned her as to where she would live and who would get the money and houses, so margery KNEW all along that Archibald was the beneficiary and she must have asked her sister WHY or even told the doctor herself. I admit it is fantastic to suspect Dr Archibald, but it is only a theory to add to the pot. Plus he made me sick that he inherited all the old girl's money but couldn't send a bunch of flowers to the funeral after he found out he was getting nearly a million quid in today's money from the Wren family. If not a bastard by birth he certainly was one in nature.

I feel his professional involvement in the case placed him above suspicion and the police should have investigated as to why he was the sole beneficiary. The police love a Masonic handshake.

Could Dr Archibald have attempted to murder Margery and then come out to attend to her injuries, threatening her quietly that he would kill her next time if she didn't keep quiet? Quite easily and she wouldn't want the truth to come out and her family to be gossiped about so she kept quiet. Don't forget how respectable Dr Harold Shipman appeared to be whilst persuading his patients to change their wills in his favour before killing over 400 people. Doctors can be murderous creatures devoid of all empathy.

Dr Archibald died in 1963. 33 years after Margery Wren. His large detached house, Cumberland Villa in Durlock Avenue, was valued at around £1,000 for probate yet he left £86,931. Obviously he managed to accumulate a great deal of money somehow in addition to that which he had inherited from Jenny, enough spare cash to have purchased an astonishing 86 large detached houses in Ramsgate (86k is over 2 million today although 86 detached Ramsgate houses would cost nearer 40 million to purchase now) and all on a back street GP's salary. Makes you wonder who else put him in their will.

Good luck to any budding Sherlock who attempts to solve this murder mystery, I think it would make a fantastic crime novel, one of the most mysterious whodunnits I have ever come across.

Here is some family research that may help any 'have-a-go' armchair detectives:

Margery Wren Born 1851 at 3 Charlotte Street, Broadstairs Kent. Parents; William Wren & Elizabeth Ann Richards. Margery's siblings were; Joseph Wren 1840, Elizabeth Ann Wren 1844, Mary-Jane (Jenny) Wren 1845-1927.

The Father William Wren was the son of John Wren & Ann Strevens. Johns other children were John, Henry, Joseph, Jane and Edward, the latter was the father of Hannah Cook mentioned in the account. Hannah Coleman Wren was born in Broadstairs in 1859 and had 7 siblings, all of which were Margery's cousins and all had children too. Hannah married Thomas Ford Cook and had 7 children including the school janitor & the London copper.

The Archibalds:

Richard James Archibald born 13 August 1877, Baptised 16th Sept 1877 at Battersea St Marks Wandsworth London, His parents were James Thomas Archibald and Charlotte Caroline Harrison. The parents address was given as 20 Auckland Road Battersea. Fathers occupation given as a solicitors clerk.

The Father James Archibald died aged 31 on 29 August 1879 when Richard was not quite 2 years old. His occupation at death was still just a clerk not a solicitor. His Father Joseph Archibald (Richard's grandfather) had been a publican who had come to London from Dorset and worked as a builder.

James Thomas Archibald had married Charlotte Caroline Harrison 18 Sep 1873 in Westminster London

Richard was their youngest and he had two older sisters, Amelia Caroline 1875-1941 and Edith Maud 1876-1946

The 1881 census records Richard 3 yrs old living at 21 Selwood Terrace Kensington with just his Mother & sisters.

The 1891 census records Richard as 13 with his mother & sisters living at 66 Moyna Rd Streatham.

The 1901 census records Richard as 23 and a medical student in Lodgings in Lambeth. Someone was paying his students fees !!

The 1911 census records Richard as 33 and a GP living at 7 Chapel Place Ramsgate. He has been married 3 years and his wife was Gertrude.

Marriage: Richard married Gertrude Florence Riddle aged 25, on 25 July 1907 at Upper Tooting London, her father was Fredrick Henry Brimble Riddle an auctioneer. Richard states his father is deceased but claims he was a solicitor (Really he was only a solicitors clerk) His address was 23 Crockerton Road Tooting and Gertrude's address was 87 Drakefield Road. The vicar seems to have been a relative of Gertrude's named AE Riddle, vicar of Todmorden Banbury.

Richard and Gertrude had two daughters.

Pamela and Iris Barbara. 1908 – 1990 died surrey aged 91

Evelyn (Kim) Phyllis. Born 1913, death unknown.

Evelyn became her father's medical secretary in the Ramsgate surgery then joined the women's Royal Navy for the war and was mostly known by her nickname Kim. After the war she moved to Westminster London and married Thomas Tatlow in 1950.

Iris married in 1934 a local Ramsgate man named John Vincent, he died in 1964

Gertrude had already died in 1955 predeceasing her husband.

Richard Archibald was 86 when he died in 1963. There were no known grandchildren.

The solicitor that administered Jenny's will was Stewart Watson Oldershaw Solicitors 43 Bedford Row Holborn.

Sources: The Advertiser 26 Sept 1930. Yorkshire Post and Leeds Intelligencer 30 September 1930. Whitstable Times and Herne Bay Herald 04 October 1930. Gloucester Citizen 30 September 1930. Plus a further selection of news reports and Ancestry.com.

Cumberland Villa (now lodge) Durlock Ave, Ramsgate
Home of Dr Archibald

D J Birkin

5 Chapel Place Ramsgate - Doctors Surgery

34.

Attempted Gassing 1935

No murder here, but definitely a foul deed.

At Kent Assizes, July 1935: Mrs Amy Gertrude Bourne, 29, of Margate, was sentenced to 3 years penal servitude for the attempted murder of her two babies by coal gas poisoning. Mr Quintin Hogg, prosecuting, told the court that Mrs Bourne lived with her children and husband in the back room of her Mother's house. Since September Mr Bourne had been out of work and the family were in receipt of 32 shillings a week in state benefits.

On June 7 Amy Bourne was depressed owing to her husband's unemployment. The husband went to the labour exchange at 2.30pm and returned at 5.10pm. He had found work and was rather keyed up. When one of the children began to cry he lost his temper and so quarrelled with his wife. (Not happy about finding a job then) He then left the house. Amy Bourne felt that life was becoming unbearable, so she locked the door and windows and turned on the gas. Mrs Bourne's mother smelt gas and got a lodger to force the door. Amy and the two babies were taken outside for fresh air and quickly recovered. PC Cory stated there were no previous convictions against the prisoner and the family were respected by their neighbours in Margate. He also said the family were all well nourished, had 32 shillings a week to live on and the woman's Mother also helped provide the family with ample food. It was not a case of terrible poverty in his opinion but one of loss of temper. A doctor who examined the children found them to be well nourished and very healthy. Mr Percy Gray defending said Mrs Bourne had temporarily lost her reason and was usually a good wife and Mother. The medical officer of Holloway prison said that the prisoner was depressed when admitted to the gaol but had since recovered and there was no sign of insanity. The judge, Mr Justice Charles was most incensed. He had not a single ounce of sympathy for Amy Bourne. He stated that all the evidence proved the children were in lovely condition and the family had more than enough to live on. The prisoner had deliberately tried to murder her babies just because she had a little tiff with her husband, in that case every time she had a little tiff no baby would be safe. He could find nothing at all to excuse what she had done.

Sentencing Amy Bourne to three years Penal servitude, the prisoner collapsed screaming "Oh. no, oh please, not that" The woman's Mother also cried out "Oh no, please don't" then also collapsed. Both women were assisted from the court. Alderman Pettman of Margate launched a public appeal for funds to help the prisoner to appeal her sentence. - No further details found.

I guess Amy did the porridge and poor old Granny Bourne had to look after the kids for 3 years. I never found out who it was that had informed the police on the family in the first place.

Penal servitude generally meant being sent to prison and being forced to do hard physical work as an extra punishment.

Source: Various contemporary accounts in the British Newspaper Archive.

35.

The Birchington Corpse 1938

Not a murder this time but a death of such bizarre local interest I have chosen to include it anyway for if you are interested in Birchington history there really is nowhere else you might expect to read about it. At least now it is recorded for posterity. I have given you the story basically as reported in the press and afterwards provided all my own research.

In Oct 1900 Mrs Frances Ward, a widow, moved into number 3 Minnis Road Birchington with her two teenage daughters. Initially she employed a young live-in maid and two local lads, on a casual basis, to do odd jobs, but apart from these people virtually no one in Birchington ever saw the three women or found out anything about them for the next 38 years. The secretive ladies kept themselves inside their locked and barred house only rarely venturing out at night for a short stroll after dark to the postbox. No callers were ever admitted to the house and tradesmen's deliveries were arranged by post with food and goods being left on the doorstep, payments were always made by postal cheques.

The two odd job chaps were trusted to be allowed inside very occasionally to do work. Naturally they told tales of how the house was maintained in a most peculiar way. All cupboards were unused and screwed shut. Provisions and processions were kept as parcels wrapped up in brown paper piled in locked rooms. Chicken wire was nailed over the house windows on the outside and the same for the conservatory as if the place was expected to soon come under siege. Surprisingly the three women liked the house to be regularly redecorated and kept fairly clean although there were newspapers piled up to the ceiling dating from 1900, the time when the family moved in (this seems to be par for the course with reclusive people) The ladies once kept a small dog in the house which was well treated. When a dog warden called to inquire about it he had to shout through the letterbox and ask to see the dog's licence, no words were exchanged and the dog licence was poked through the letterbox and then snatched back again. This eccentric but contented life of female isolation came to a sudden end on 13 July 1938 when one of the employed men, David Hutchings, by now a middle aged man, was invited into the house to do a repair job. He had recently redecorated one of the bedrooms, unlocked for the occasion, and was used to all other rooms being padlocked up. He was also used to not seeing the ladies of the house even when inside as they would pass him instructions by note and scurry away like mice. On this occasion he did not inquire into the absence of the Mother, who was now in her 80s and quite frail, he guessed she was in the house somewhere.

As David went about his job he noticed the padlock on one of the bedroom doors had been left undone and being an inquisitive chap he popped his head round the door to be nosey. The room stunk of camphor squares piled around the bed in which was a body shaped lump covered in a sheet. When he lifted the bottom of the sheet he saw a stiff white leg. Poor David left the house faster than a rat up a drainpipe. Soon the police and a police surgeon, Dr Bowie, were on the Ward's doorstep requesting entry to the house. A large crowd quickly gathered in the street outside hoping for a glimpse of the mysterious women. They were to be disappointed. When an ambulance arrived to remove the old lady's corpse the daughters had already left the premises with the police and had gone into hiding. The daughters, Beatrice and Gertrude Ward, know to their mother as Maud and Jane for some unknown reason, told police that their mother had taken ill at Christmas 1937 with influenza, took to her bed on 12 March and refused most food, she had finally died on 21 April 1938 at 6am. She had insisted on not seeing a doctor and the daughters said they did not know of a doctor anyway as they had never used one. The daughters had cared attentively for their sick mother but had not wanted to put her in the wet ground with insects and had not wanted to involve other people and that is why they had kept her corpse for the last 3 months and would have kept it forever if they had not been found out.

3 Minnis Road Birchington

An inquest was held in Margate a few days later where it was found that the daughters were in their 50s and had been kept virtually prisoners by their Mother all of their lives. The women had also promised to not bury their Mother because she had had a morbid dread of being buried alive.

Miss Beatrice said she had seen whom she believed to have been her father in London twice when she was about 6 years old. She believed that he was an independent gentleman possible named John Ward and a doctor in the Army. She was later told by her Mother that he had died in 1895 following an accident.

The family did not observe birthdays and the women did not know when they were born or exactly how old they were, or how old their mother was. After they moved to Birchington they had never left the village and rarely the house. They believed they were of the upper classes and knew no persons of their own class in Birchington with whom to associate with.

The trip to Margate for the inquest was very traumatic for the two distressed middle aged spinsters. They were dressed in deep black mourning with veils – the clothing had kindly been arranged for the ladies by David Hutchings wife. Miss Beatrice threatened to sue the newspaper reporters in the courtroom if they published her words! (Of course they published as it is not illegal to report on inquests) Miss Beatrice continued. "We have never seen our birth certificates, if indeed they exist, and this is causing problems with the trustees who are administering our mother's money which we think comes from our mother's family, but now we have nothing and as mother did not leave a will we don't know what we shall live on." The sister's said they had now engaged a solicitor to sort out the house and money to see that it didn't go to their mother's relatives and leave them destitute and homeless. (luckily they were granted full probate a few months later.)

The coroner concluded that Mrs Frances Ward had died of unknown, but probable natural causes, but he could not allow her death to be registered as the wife of John Ward as there was no evidence to support any marriage. However there was evidence that her real name was Florence Matilda Greatrex.

After the inquest the body was released for burial and the daughters said their Mother had once expressed the notion that if she should have to be buried at some time then she wished to be interred in Hove cemetery in Sussex next to her best friend Dr Dill. David Hutchings kindly went to Hove and made sure this was OK with the doctor Dill's wife, which apparently it was. (mysterious) The funeral then took place on 23 July 1938.

The doctor in question was John Frederick Gordon Dill who had died back in 1925 aged 66. The Hutchings and a few others, including a policeman from Birchington, also attended the burial to support the sisters, who were very weak and distressed. Mourners included a Miss Rowley from Hove who told Daily Mail reporters that she had visited the Wards a few times over the years with her father on business and found them to be very nice people. Last time she visited she was told the mother was in Ramsgate. She had no idea the old lady was dead upstairs. Miss Rowley's father, William Rowley, had been a trustee of the old lady's finances.

When the old lady's body had first been discovered the sisters had sought refuge from the crowds of gawpers by staying with David Hutchings and his wife Lillian at 7 Westfield Road Birchington and there they remained, never going back to the Minnis Rd house. A year later when the Minnis Rd house had been sold the two sisters were able to buy another house called Green Roof, 27 Danes Rd Birchington. They bought this house for David Hutchings and his wife and lived there with them as they were incapable of living alone. Sadly Gertrude could not adapt to life without her mother and had a complete mental collapse and lost her mind. She had to be put into a care home in Birchington where she lived for another incredible 30 years before dying in 1971. Beatrice on the other hand adapted to her new life wonderfully, she blossomed in fact and remained part of the Hutchings family becoming a much loved 'Aunty Bea' to the Hutchings children and grandchildren. Several photos I have seen of the Hutchings family show Beatrice to be a kindly looking matronly lady smiling in the company of other women and lots of children. She was said to be great fun and loved kids. I was pleased to know she ended up having a happy life being adopted by the Hutchings family.

Gertrude Ward died in 1971 at Birchington with the birth date of 1895 instead of 1887....actually she was 84 and didn't know.

Beatrice Ward died in 1976 away from home in Walsall Staffordshire whilst visiting a daughter of the Hutchings family, her date of birth given as 1892 instead of 1886....actually she was 90. Both sisters were buried next to their mother in Hove cemetery in Sussex.

Beatrice left an estate of £40,000 mostly to the Hutchings family but she also left £10,000 to be distributed amongst any elderly residents of Birchington who were over 75.

What a sweet lady she was.

I then did my own detective work and this is what I discovered: The 1939 census recorded the daughters correct details as:

Beatrice Sarah Greatrex Ward born Paddington 22 Feb 1886 and Gertrude Victoria Greatrex Ward born Paddington 12 Jan 1887.

Their births were not registered, the surname of Ward seems to have been an invented surname their mother gave them to hide their illegitimacy.

The mother, who claimed to be a Mrs Ward, was in truth born Florence Matilda Greatrex in Brighton in 1855, actually aged 83 at death. Florence's parents were not married either and at some point Florence went to live with her father Edward Greatrex in Croydon when she was still a child.

Edward Greatrex (the mother's own father) b1796 in Derby, was a surgeon in the Royal Coldstream Guards obtaining the rank of Major. He was sent to Barbados and whilst there was court-martialed on 1st Oct 1827 and dishonourably discharged for fighting. He was then immediately reinstated at the same court as his conduct regarding his medical work was excellent and basically the army were short of good surgeons. He was already 59 years old when Florence was born in 1855. In 1859 he married for the first time (so he professed) when aged 65, to a woman called Sarah Tyler who was also a single parent with a grown up son named Edward Tyler born 1839 in Berkshire (was she Florence's real mother and was Edward really Edward's son? His birth certificate. Says father Edward Tyler but Sarah wasn't married and Tyler was her maiden name) Edward Greatrex then retired from the army and moved to 1 Torriano Villas Broadstairs with his daughter Florence, son/stepson Edward and new wife Sarah. He died at Broadstairs in 1882 aged 83 or 88 years, it seems he couldn't remember how old he was either - actually he was 86. He left his house and money to his wife Sarah. The stepson Edward, a sailor, then died in 1885 and Sarah Greatrex moved to Bournemouth. It seems this is when Florence fell out with her mother/stepmother over her being an unmarried mum with two little girls and Sarah and Florence never spoke again, which seems very hypocritical of Sarah as Florence and Edward were both born out of wedlock, but perhaps Florence never knew that. When Sarah died in 1908 she left her Bournemouth property to Florence in the end which suggests maybe she was her real mother and that there was a legitimate reason that Edward couldn't marry her when she had Florence. (I suggest that Edward was already married, separated and couldn't get a divorce, he then finally married Sarah when his wife eventually died.) As Florence had lived at 3

Minnis Rd since 1900 it proves she had somehow purchased the house before inheriting her mothers money in 1908.

It is difficult to piece this dysfunctional family together. After her father's death in 1882 Florence disappeared and neither she nor her two young daughters appear on the 1891 census. When they turn up on the 1901 census they are already living at 3 Minnis Rd Birchington and the family had changed their names to Ward.

The Mother was now calling herself Frances Ward a widow and gave her daughters names as Maud Ward (not Beatrice) and Jane Ward (not Gertrude) she also mysteriously claimed to have been born in Tunbridge Wells Kent, which she was not.

Then on the 1911 census for 3 Minnis Rd, Florence Greatrex gave her name as Frances Ward again but reverted to being born at Brighton Sussex and again gave her daughters names as Maud and Jane Ward but removed 8 years from the girls ages and 17 years from her own. Florence Greatrex was definitely trying to hide her identity. Did she not want any relatives to discover she was an unmarried mum? It was considered extremely shameful in the past, especially in the middle classes, but this seems more than that, this is an expression of mental paranoia. Clearly the poor woman had a breakdown when her lover died and it would seem she was left to deal with that illness alone.

I then wondered why Florence would request burial in Sussex next to Dr John Fredrick Gordon Dill and why the doctor's wife would agree to this strange request. I discovered what I believe is the answer to the mysterious identity of the father of the Ward girls. Of course one can never fully prove it but all things added together the brother of Dr Dill seems to be the chap in the frame. He was Robert Charles Gordon Dill, born 1861 in Brighton, same place as Florence. Robert, like his brother and father, also became a doctor. He joined the army and became a surgeon in Westminster at the same Army hospital as Florence's dad. Dr Robert Dill then had some kind of terrible accident in 1895 in London and died from his injuries in April 1895 at his Father's country house Downey Court, Cosham in Hampshire, where he had been conveyed for recuperation. A notice of his death appeared in the newspapers explaining that he had finally succumbed to illness following an accident. A living member of the Hutchings family still (2020) remembers Beatrice well and was told that Beatrice believed her mysterious father was run over by carriage in the street in London and when told of this her Mother, Florence, was seen screaming and running hysterically about in the street. These facts then seem to fit the vague story the two daughters were told of their father's identity and John Ward was simply a made-up name to protect the identity of their father really being Dr Robert Dill and deflect gossip away from the Dill family who were very upper class snobs. One can only assume the brother, Dr John Dill, had acted as mediator between the parties and kindly assisted Florence with her two little girls after his brother's death and that is why she considered him to be her best friend. Major Surgeon John Dill's wife, Mary Kathlene, then knew all about her husband's benevolent actions and had no objection to the funeral arrangements. John Dill was the eldest son of the Dill family. The fact that Robert and Florence were never married seems to be a case of his parents disapproving and possibly threatening to disinherit him.

The Dill family were Old money, their men all being Army majors even generals, the daughters had all been presented at court and featured on the lists of débutantes. All the Dills made very advantageous marriages. A childhood sweetheart from the wrong side of the village fence was not going to be an acceptable wife. Robert's parents were no doubt hoping he would make a financially advantageous marriage too and had been funding their son with an allowance that he simply couldn't do without as he secretly had Flo and the kids to support on Army pay, so the poor lad must have felt trapped between the devil and the deep blue sea.

Robert's parents were probably genuinely shocked to find out that their son had two illegitimate daughters in London aged 8 and 9 years and I doubt very much if poor Florence was allowed to go down to Hampshire to be with Robert as he lay dying. I can imagine not knowing how he was faring must have been the start of her mental illness.

Captain Dr Robert Dill was buried in a family plot at St John the Evangelist's Church burial ground, Burgess Hill, Sussex. Begrudgingly the Dill family did quietly support Florence financially after the death of their son with regular payments and it was no doubt they who purchased the Minnis Road house to ensure Florence's silence. I think if Florence had discovered where Robert was buried she would have requested burial next to him, I suspect the family had always refused to tell her less she should have kept turning up and making a spectacle of herself at the graveside in front of his relatives.

Robert's father was a General and surgeon in the Army whilst his Mother Augusta Dill lived to be 100 years and was the daughter of General Sir Charles Wale a close friend and comrade of the Duke of Wellington. Obviously such posh and well connected people made no attempt to acknowledge their two illegitimate granddaughters as part of their own family.

Too embarrassing to explain to the neighbours I guess.

I do this family research for a lot of cases not just because I'm a nosey beak who loves a mystery but also to help fellow genealogists who are interested in discovering more of their own family history. Ordinary people are often far more interesting than famous celebrities.

I'd like to thank a relation of the Hutchings family who was kind enough to help me fill in the gaps and show me her family photos, thank you Gillian x it's lovely to know that Beatrice had such loving friends when she needed them.

Sources: Thanet Advertiser 15 July 1938. Nottingham Evening Post 6 October 1938. Nottingham Journal 19 July 1938. Thanet Advertiser 19 & 29 July 1938. Daily Mirror 23 July 1938. Aberdeen Evening Express 28 May 1976. Daily Mirror 28 January 1976 plus assorted news reports and Ancestry.com

Minnis Road: The word 'minnis' is believed to derive from the Saxon word (ge)maennes, which means common land used as pasture.

General Sir Charles Wale: Great grandfather of Beatrice and Gertrude. He has a wikipedia page plus here is his portrait and bio. **http://www.artwarefineart.com/gallery/portrait-general-sir-sir-charles-wale-kcb-1763%E2%80%931845**

Thomas Wale Great great Grandfather of Beatrice and Gertrude **https://en.wikipedia.org/wiki/Thomas_Wale**

Robert Dill had three brothers and two sisters , Aunts and uncles to Beatrice and Gertrude, the most famous was Author Mildred Darby who lived at Leap Castle, here's the link

https://en.wikipedia.org/wiki/Mildred_Darby

It is such a shame that the two girls grew up knowing nothing of their interesting relations and illustrious lineage.

36.

Scarred for Life 1940

Doris Todd and George Sylvester Cooke, 26, were both natives of Liverpool. They had courted for a while but after many quarrels Doris had ended their relationship. She joined the A.T.S to get away and was stationed in Margate. On the 7 April George found out where Doris was and came to Margate to find her. Once found he slashed her five times across the face with his penknife, one of the wounds so deep that Doris was permanently disfigured. George was caught and sentenced to 12 months imprisonment. It was found out that he had served a sentence for malicious wounding before in 1935 in Liverpool.

Source: Thanet Advertiser 28 June 1940

37.

Minster Child Sexually Abused 1940

At the Summer Assizes in Maidstone 1940, Norman Pearson, 23, a dairyman, was sentenced to six months hard labour, twice. He was guilty of sexually interfering, twice, with an 11 year old girl at Minster in Thanet.

The Judge, Sir James Cassels said, "it is a case so serious I would like to give you penal servitude for life. But I am bound by the law. Nothing can mitigate what you did, it is idle of you to have said that it was the child who had tempted you!"

(Typical claim by paedophiles)

Source: Thanet Advertiser 28 June 1940

38.

She didn't like Boys 1941

Nothing much ever happened in Birchington. When the local dustman went missing for a few days the whole village could talk of nothing else, so imagine the tongues wagging when residents discovered that a woman pushing a pram around their streets had walked up to the Birchington policeman and declared

"My baby is dead. Look in the pram. I did it, I killed it."

On 11 Sept 1941, Mrs Mary Hogben, aged 40, of Gordon Square Birchington, gave birth to her fifth child. Mary was married to an aircraft man in the R.A.F and the couple already had 4 daughters aged between 4 and 16 years. They had not planned for another child. When the child, a boy, Michael Frederick, had been born, Mary Hogben had fallen into a deep depression. It had never crossed her mind she might have a boy, Mary assumed she would have another girl like before. She declared that she didn't like boys and had no idea what to do with a boy as she was only used to having girls around her. Mary's family thought she was being silly and would just get used to having a son and learn to cope. She didn't. Mary's irrational fear of the boy escalated until she was out of her mind with anxiety.

There were several air raids over Birchington at the time and this didn't help to calm Mary down. On the 25 Nov Mary had stayed in bed until the afternoon. Her husband was home and concerned with how depressed his wife was. At 5.30pm Mary said she would go for a walk with the baby in his pram to get some fresh air. Baby Michael was now 11 weeks old.

Birchington on Sea c1920

After Mary left the house she just pushed her baby aimlessly around the streets of Birchington. She was in a daze. When several hours had passed and Mary had not returned home, her worried husband set out to look for her. Birchington is a small place, but still he couldn't find his wife and reported her missing to the local policeman on the beat who agreed to look out for her. Mr Hogben returned home to look after his daughters.

At 10.40pm, in Canterbury Road, PC Colyer saw a woman answering to Mary Hogben's description heading towards him with a pram. That's when Mary told him she had killed her baby.

At that moment Mr Hogben arrived, he had come out to look for his wife again as he was frantic with worry. Mary on the other hand was very calm as if in a zombie like state. She said to both the PC and her husband. "I tied a nappy round his head and killed him. He would not stop crying. He was born in an air raid and there have been air raids ever since. They would have killed him anyway."

The shocked policeman grabbed the baby from the pram and ran to his police box where he attempted to revive the infant with the kiss of life but to no avail. (good man for trying) The police surgeon was then summoned and he took the child away.

Mary, accompanied by her distraught husband, were escorted to the police station where Mary made a statement and was arrested. She said she was very sorry but she couldn't cope with the boy any longer. She remembered tying the nappy over his head at some point after leaving the house, but had no idea how many hours had passed since then.

At the coroner's inquest and later at Margate Magistrate's court, it was shown that Mary had been an excellent Mother to her 4 daughters and a good capable wife, but the air raids had shattered her nerves and she had been tipped, irrationally, over the edge by the birth of her son. The verdict was death by asphyxiation and Mary was indicted for the murder of her child. When asked if she understood the indictment Mary said feebly "Yes, can I go home now?" The Judge gently replied "Best not for the moment."

At Mary Hogben's trial it was shown her state of mind had greatly improved whilst rested in prison and she now fully understood the seriousness of the crime she had committed. Her state of mind at the time she committed the murder was taken into account and the charge was reduced to manslaughter, to which Mary pleaded guilty. She was sentenced to 6 months imprisonment with the order that she receive mental health treatment whilst in prison.

Sources: Thanet Advertiser 28 Nov 1941 and 2 & 12 Dec 1941 & 13 Jan 1942

39.

Wicked Mother Drowned her Son 1946

Lillian Iris Dowsell thought she was dying, no apparent medical symptoms, it was just a feeling she had. The press described her as, 25, a housewife of Sydney Road Ramsgate.

Lillian took her 6 year old son Nigel Anthony Dowsell for a walk on the beach on the night of Good Friday at 11pm. There she pushed his head into the waves and held him there until he was drowned. The murderous Mother then carried the dead child home.

The landlady of the Ramsgate boardinghouse where Lillian lived, Mrs Hewett, saw Lillian return carrying the wet boy and confronted her. A Nurse, Mrs Noble, who lived nearby, was fetched and pronounced the boy dead.

When asked why she had killed her son, Lillian replied, "I loved him so but I didn't want to leave him behind. I couldn't breath and I know I will die soon the same as my Mother died."

Lillian Dowsell was later found unfit to plead at the Old Bailey as she had since gone completely insane. The Judge ordered she be securely detained at his Majesty's pleasure (Most likely Broadmoor) for an undetermined period.

Sources: Thanet Advertiser 14 May 1946: Thanet Advertiser & Echo 28 May 1946

40.

Copper tries to kill Wife 1947

A special improvised magistrates court was held in a ward of Ramsgate hospital in 1947. Propped up on pillows, Mr Charles Hall, 53, retired policeman, of South Eastern Rd Ramsgate, was charged with felonious wounding his wife, Edith Regina Hall, with intent to murder her on the 23 May. Charles was further charged with attempting suicide by cutting his own throat. (Suicide was then illegal)

The court was told that when Charles Hall was apprehended at the scene of his crime he appeared very dazed and clutching his own throat had asked the police "What's happened. Who did this to me?"

The court was adjourned until the 20th June when Charles Hall was sufficiently recovered to be brought before Ramsgate Magistrates Court escorted by two officers. Mr Hall, who was once himself a Metropolitan Police officer, was allowed to sit as he was still weak. The wife, Edith, said the couple had two children, 16 & 8 years old, and their married life had always been a happy one. She thought it should never have come to court as theirs was a tragedy of the war.

The surgeon at Ramsgate hospital deposed that Mrs Hall had been admitted in a state of shock with cuts to her skull and fingers caused by an axe. Mr Hall had been admitted with a slit throat and was violent and had to be restrained.

Edith Hall said in court that she didn't want to give evidence against her husband. When told that, in this instant, she must but it was just a formality. Edith then said her husband had been acting a bit strange for a long time and on the 21 May she had gone with him to see a psychologist in Margate because of his nerves. The next day he couldn't concentrate. "I was going to buy some potatoes," she said "so I put on my coat. As I bent down to pick up my basket Charlie hit me over the head. I put my hands to my head and he hit me again with the wood chopper cutting my fingers. I managed to get out of the house and ran to my neighbours for help."

Edith told the court that her husband was a good man, he had been a Police officer for 30 years and had been awarded the Kings Police medal for gallantry when they lived in Bromley in 1922. She said her husband's nerves had been bad since they were bombed out. He had gone to a mental hospital for 10 days and was then medically discharged from the Police Service with his nerves.

Edith Hall cried in court as she told what a wonderful husband Charles was and how he had never hurt anyone before in his life. Charles also sobbed in court telling his wife how sorry he was and that he loved her very much. The case was passed to the next Assizes and Charles was granted permission for his children to visit him in prison.

On Tues 24 June at Maidstone Assizes Charles presented a dismal sight in the dock, a weak and broken shell of a man. Doctor H Grierson of Brixton prison where Charles had been held, immediately made a statement that Charles Hall was now certifiably insane and certainly unfit to plead. The Judge ordered Charles Hall to be securely detained at his Majesty's pleasure in Broadmoor for an undetermined period, for his own good.

Source: Thanet Advertiser 27 May 1947: Thanet Advertiser 13, 20 and 27 June 1947.

41.

Husband hits wife with Axe 1949

William Henry Stewart, 66, retired painter & decorator of 120 Southwood Rd Ramsgate, made his appearance before Ramsgate magistrates on Mon 5 Sept 1949 charged with the attempted murder of his wife Hester Jane Stewart on 17 August.

Stewart, weak on his feet, was allowed to sit on a chair and held his cap nervously in his hands. Stewart recalled how on the morning in question he took a cup of tea to his wife in her bedroom about 6.30am, as he always did. She then pulled a face at him and made a rude gesture to him with two fingers. Without thinking he went and fetched a hand axe from the garden and returned to his wife's bedroom where he hit her twice on the head, she was not badly hurt and screamed out for their adult son, also called William, who immediately ran in and took the axe away.

Mr Stewart, who was very deaf, said "I told my son to call the police as I thought I had gone mad. My wife is an evil woman who has made my life a misery, she wants nothing but money. I hit her in the heat of the moment, I wish I was dead. My wife treats me like dirt, our son gets eggs and bacon but I only get bread and margarine. She makes me do the cleaning and wash the clothes. My life with her is unbearable. Please Sir let me die."

It was stated that Mrs Stewart had been taken to Ramsgate Hospital where she received 5 stitches for a cut in her head, an x-ray showed no other damage but she was kept in for a week in case she had had concussion. (A week for observation! Plenty of hospital beds in those days)

At Kent Assizes in November the Judge, Mr Justice Croom Johnson, remarked that Mr Stewart's case was a very sad one. He noted that William Stewart was only 66, but thought he looked a hundred. The defence said that Mr Stewart had always been a very respectable man and was now suffering from premature senile decay (dementia) and had been very ill used by his wife. His Wife and son had since disowned him and he had no other family to care for him. It was suggested that it might be better for Mr Stewart's health if he was placed in a mental hospital. The Judge thought that Stewart's state of mind made him unsuitable for an asylum where he could just wander out again and thought a secure criminal hospital was a better option for him. He ordered that William Stewart be confined to Broadmoor for three years where he could be medically supervised. (poor old chap) I expect he went completely mad in Broadmoor.

Sources: Thanet Advertiser & Echo 5 Sep 1949:

42.

The Broadstairs Flasher 1950

On 31 January, at Broadstairs, a baker's delivery man exposed himself to two little girls aged only 5 and 7 years. The man was delivering bread in a van in Northwood Road when the outrage occurred. Fortunately, Norman Duncan Hurworth, 23, of Nelson Crescent Ramsgate was immediately apprehended by residents. When taken before the local magistrates on 27 Feb Hurworth admitted the lewd act. He had previously been convicted for flashing in Ramsgate in 1948. The prisoner said he was humiliated and asked if he might have medical advice. The Judge sentenced Hurworth to three months in prison.

Sources: Thanet Advertiser 28 Feb 1950:

43.

She threw her Babies in the Harbour 1950

Mrs Amelia Leach, 33, of Paragon Street Ramsgate, appeared before Ramsgate Magistrates on 16 February 1950 charged with attempting to murder her 2 sons by throwing them into the sea at Ramsgate Harbour. Amelia appeared smartly dressed in a long green coat and black shoes but without a hat. (Apparently the public thought the lack of hat to be shocking)

Her young sons, William James Albert Leach aged 1 year 11 months and David Anthony Leach aged 10 months, had been rescued from the attempt to drown them and were in Ramsgate Hospital in a satisfactory condition.

Mrs Frances Fincham, a yachtswoman, said she saw Amelia Leach throw the babies into the sea. Mr Thomas Harris, bus driver, and Mr Reginald Mills, postman, both dived into the harbour and rescued the children. (Good men)

In her defence Mrs Leach rambled "I was married in 1948 but I have never been happy with my husband, we quarrelled. I now live in a cottage with a kitchen where we eat. I bought a coconut and it was bad so I took it back and the man was really nasty to me so I went to the harbour and threw the children in. There were plenty of people around so I knew they would only get a chill."

It was clear the woman was mentally confused. She was removed to an asylum to be assessed. Amelia Leach was later found unfit to plead at the Assizes as she was declared insane. The Judge ordered she be securely detained at the King's pleasure in Broadmoor Asylum.

With a little extra research I then discovered that six years later on 2 July 1956 there was an outbreak of food poisoning in the women's wing at Broadmoor from contaminated meat. 67 female patients suffered chronic gastroenteritis. Amelia Leach was one of two inmates that died in extreme agony from the poisoned meat. Hopefully her children were adopted and looked after kindly.

Sources: Thanet Advertiser 21 Feb 1950: Leicester Daily Mercury 20 March 1950:

Birmingham Daily Post - Thursday 12 July 1956.

44.

The Murder of Lillian Chubb 1958

In February 1958, a bus driver, proceeding along Hugin Avenue Broadstairs, spotted a pair of legs poking out of a hedge. The police were notified and discovered the body of a woman, the lady was fully dressed in a green coat and fur boots but her handbag was missing. She appeared to have been strangled.

Seven days later, after a large police search of the neighbourhood, it was discovered that the dead woman actually lived in Hugin Ave. (Good police search)

Someone who thought the description sounded familiar came forward and identified the body as Miss Lillian Chubb, 52, who worked in a nearby store.

Lillian had lived with her Brother Ernest Chubb, a plumber, 49, and his wife Edith Chubb, 46, and their 5 children. When police went to the house Edith Chubb immediately admitted that she had killed her sister in law Lillian.

Mr Chubb was still at work and returned to find his wife had been taken to the police station and a policewoman was cooking the children's dinner. (Policewomen used to be nice) Mr Chubb ran to the police station to see his wife but was refused as she was under arrest.

(I wonder where Ernest thought his sister had gone all week)

When the case finally came to court Edith said that she was exhausted as she was a nurse who got up at 4am every morning for work, looked after a household of eight people with no help from anyone and had not had a break or holiday in the eighteen years she had been married. Her sister in law, Lillian, lodged with them. Lillian only paid them 21 shillings (One pound, one shilling) a week out of her £9 a week wages for her board and expected her meals too for that money. Lillian had refused to help with the cleaning or the cooking and treated Edith like her personal servant. Edith said, "Lillian was sitting at the table refusing to lift a finger when suddenly I had an impulse to just pull the ends of the yellow scarf that was wrapped around her neck and make her shut up." When Edith realised her sister in law had stopped breathing and had died, she panicked knowing that her husband was due home, so she wheeled the body of her sister in law in a barrow up the road and tipped her into the bushes. She had forgotten the handbag was still at home.

Mrs Edith Chubb leaving Hugin Avenue with two detectives

On Friday 2 May 1958, Edith Chubb was found guilty at the Old Bailey only of the manslaughter of Lillian Chubb, as Edith had shown no prior intent to commit murder and had unintentionally killed Lillian in the heat of the moment. She was sent to Holloway Women's prison for 4 years. (very lenient) A tearful Mr Chubb said he loved his wife and wished he had helped her more with the children and the chores. He had no idea she was at her wits end. He promised his wife that things would be better when she was released and he would make it up to her. As Edith was taken away to the cells she called out to her husband "Just look after the children Ernie."

Sources: Daily Mail 8 & 15 Feb & 3 May 1958 and assorted papers in the British newspaper Archive.

Well that's it for Thanet.

If I have left you with a taste for more grisly Kent history then please look out for future titles in my Kent murders and Foul deeds series.

Printed in Great Britain
by Amazon